Inspiring Wonder, Awe, and Empathy

Praise for *Inspiring Wonder, Awe, and Empathy*

"A richly told story of how our spiritual awakening happens early on in life and how play and nature serve as positive forces that offer spiritual gifts to enjoy throughout our lifetime. This book is a series of revelations, a narrative easy to enjoy and learn much from. It's a lovely book!" —Walter F. Drew, EdD, cofounder and executive director, Institute for Self Active Education

"Dr. Schein offers us a provocative new lens for examining child development and exploring the inner world of the child. Her perspective on spirituality encourages and challenges us to slow down and be present in moments of joy and wonder with the children we care for. She grounds her thinking in both foundational and contemporary theories and provides readers with practical suggestions to support them in nurturing this important trait in children." —Robin Ploof, cofacilitator of NAEYC's Play Policy and Practice Interest Forum

"*Inspiring Wonder, Awe, and Empathy* gives language to an important and new way to look at an aspect of development in young children that has previously been misunderstood or overlooked. This book is thoughtful and thought provoking, giving new insight to children's spiritual growth from infancy on." —Susan Remick Topek, early childhood consultant

"Dr. Schein's book is an inspiring and refreshing approach to children's spirituality, highlighting love and reminding us of its center stage status in early childhood education. This book makes a significant contribution to the field of children's spiritual development." —Jennifer Mata-McMahon, EdD, author of *Spiritual Experiences in Early Childhood Education*

"Dr. Schein has successfully unpacked the meaning of spirituality for young children in this incredibly compelling and well-written treatise that will engage early childhood educators, parents, and leaders in the field. Far beyond another teacher's guide, this book touches the very soul of early childhood education." —Dr. David Brody, coordinator, Early Childhood Education, Efrata College of Education, Jerusalem

"Dr. Schein has written an extraordinary book. It contains essential elements, important research, and actionable ideas for intentionally supporting children's spiritual development—the missing link for creating a better world. It's a timely and important topic that all teachers and parents of young children need to read. I highly recommend it." —Patti Bailie, PhD, assistant professor, Early Childhood Education, University of Maine–Farmington

"*Inspiring Wonder, Awe, and Empathy* is a monumental addition to the field of early childhood education. Schein has fitted the missing piece of the puzzle to the development of the whole child by defining spirituality as 'reflecting deep connections and moments of wonder.' Dr. Schein makes us comfortable with the word and gives us the language and tools to bring this universal experience to any setting in any environment." —Robyn Hurvitz and Lynne Lieberman, director of professional development and senior director, Friedman Commission for Jewish Education

"In an almost magical way, Dr. Schein weaves strands of research with personal stories to illustrate how spiritual development unifies and energizes all other areas of child development. Readers will find in this engaging book new insights into spirituality and how it's manifested in children's everyday discoveries and interactions. While *Inspiring Wonder, Awe, and Empathy* addresses a serious topic, it will leave readers feeling uplifted." —Ruth Wilson, PhD, research library curator, Children and Nature Network, author of *Learning Is in Bloom* and *Nature and Young Children*

Inspiring Wonder, Awe, and Empathy

Spiritual Development in Young Children

Deborah Schein, PhD

Redleaf Press®
www.redleafpress.org
800-423-8309

Published by Redleaf Press
10 Yorkton Court
St. Paul, MN 55117
www.redleafpress.org

First edition 2017
Cover design by Erin Kirk New
Cover photograph by bst2012/stock.adobe.com
Interior design by Louise OFarrell
Typeset in Garamond Premier Pro
Interior photos on pages 13, 19, 23, 37, 80, and 123 by Johanna Resnick Rosen;
27 by Kara Lomen; 83 by Becky Surtshin; 125 by Edyta Linek/stock.adobe
.com
Images on pages 9, 20, and 134–38 by Jim Handrigan
Printed in the United States of America

24 23 22 21 20 19 18 17   1 2 3 4 5 6 7 8

Library of Congress Cataloging-in-Publication Data
Names: Schein, Deborah L., author.
Title: Inspiring wonder, awe, and empathy : spiritual development in young
    children / Deborah Schein, PhD.
Description: First edition. | St. Paul, MN : Redleaf Press, [2018] | Includes
    bibliographical references and index.
Identifiers: LCCN 2017022211 (print) | LCCN 2017036409 (ebook) |
    ISBN 9781605544854 (ebook) | ISBN 9781605544847 (pbk. :acid-free
    paper)
Subjects: LCSH: Children—Religious life. | Spirituality. | Religious
    education of children.
Classification: LCC BL625.5 (ebook) | LCC BL625.5 .S34 2018 (print) | DDC
    204.083—dc23
LC record available at https://lccn.loc.gov/2017022211

To my husband, Jeffrey Schein, who has been my support, my confidant, my walking dictionary and thesaurus, and my teacher for over forty-six years. This book would not exist without his presence and voice in my life.

Many others have been there for me during the writing of this book. I would like to pass on this blessing from my heart:

Thank you for relationships, words, and ideas,
for dialogue, experiences, and playfulness of thought.
Thank you for wonder and beauty,
and thank you for a life filled with love.

Contents

Acknowledgments

Way back when this book was just a thought, Tamar Jacobson introduced me to one of the editors of Redleaf Press. Then Mimi Plevin-Foust helped me to prepare the book proposal so that Redleaf Press might see the importance and possibility for publishing a book on spiritual development. I thank Tamar, Mimi, Kyra Ostendorf, Kara Lomen, David Heath, and Laurie Herrmann for believing in both the topic of spiritual development and in me! I also received so much support and guidance from Meredith Burks, Jim Handrigan, Sue Ostfield, and everyone else at Redleaf Press. Thank you to Louise OFarrell for providing the beautiful design of this book. Then there are others, such as my sister Lori Goodman, my friend Katie Cahn, and my blog designers and managers, Halle and Benjamin Barnett, who have all inspired me and helped me to work through the hard parts. A big thank-you goes out to my doctoral adviser, Amie Beckett, to whom I will always be grateful for sticking with me through thick and thin. Somehow, I am miraculously here at this point—writing a book. I have been given assistance from two amazing editors, Danny Miller and Heidi Hogg. I am quite sure that their gentle guidance has helped to make this book more accessible and clear for readers. Thank you also to Ester Leutenberg, who recently coauthored a book with me; she and I created pages and pages of ideas for educators and parents to use for nurturing children's spiritual development. Some of these ideas are located at the end of each chapter of this book. Finally, thank you to all the educators, directors, photographers, and colleagues I have met over the years at workshops, talks, and conferences. A special thanks goes out to Johanna Resnick Rosen, Jo Rosen photography. It is because of all of you and your support that I am able to be here, in this moment, thanking all of you.

What Is Spiritual Development for Young Children?

THIS BOOK OFFERS a new way of thinking about child development by defining spiritual development for early childhood classrooms. In pioneering a new working definition of spiritual development that begins at birth and by offering a series of strategies that can nurture a young child's spiritual development, this book initiates a dialogue that recognizes and builds on the spiritual lives of children in the classroom setting. My hope is that this dialogue will help parents and educators learn how to offer all children a stronger beginning to a rich and fulfilling life that is filled with important learning opportunities and deep connections. At one time in my professional career, I believed that spiritual development was missing in most early childhood programs. I have since come to see that it is not missing—the problem is that we do not know how to define spirituality without referencing God or religion, and we do not yet recognize it as its own domain of development.

The pages of this book are filled with my own personal experiences, the experiences of many other early childhood educators, research findings from a variety of sources, and the findings that emerged from my own social constructivist / grounded theory research study—incorporating the voices of the researcher and the participants as they respond to shared questions around topics that have not been fully explored. Our topic of spiritual development among young children led to a shared understanding of spirituality that reflects deep connections and moments of wonder rather than a focus on God and religion. This simple yet significant shift makes the topic of spiritual development accessible to all educators and for all children. In other words, the research study produced a definition of spiritual development that can be used in public school education in a way that honors and respects the separation of church and state.

When I would talk to other educators about my research in spiritual development, I was often greeted with comments such as "Can't you call it something else?" The consensus was that the language of spirituality made many teachers and other adults very uncomfortable in the school setting. Many of the study participants shared that they had never been asked to discuss spiritual development and they did not really know how to respond. I would say, "What do you think your children feel internally when you provide them with something they really love?" "Oh," they would say, "I have lots of stories about that."

Thinking a lot about Vygotsky's theory of thought and language, where one's language helps to guide one's thinking, I also began to ask myself and others a myriad of questions: What are educators, parents, and children missing when the words *spirituality* or *spiritual development* are excluded from our lexicon as we work with young children? How might spirituality be defined in a way that is more acceptable to US educators and nonreligious parents? What unfolds in this book is a new definition of spiritual development that uses familiar language, such as *love, attachment, self-awareness, disposition*, and *deep connections*.

Tracing the Question of Spiritual Development

I have been interested in exploring spiritual development for most of my life, but I can trace my decision to research a way to define spiritual development in the context of early childhood education to a specific moment in time.

Before I talk about that, I'd like to describe some of the personal experiences that led me to the topic of spiritual development. My teaching career began in 1972 with Montessori training and some amazing years as a Montessori educator. My Montessori training occurred a few years after I received a bachelor of science in psychology from the University of California at Santa Barbara (UCSB) and included training from both the American Montessori Society (AMS) and the Association Montessori Internationale (AMI). What most attracted me to the Montessori philosophy was the respect given to children; the beauty of the materials; the investigation of nature through the study of leaves, animals, plant growth, and food preparation; and the simplicity and authenticity of the learning environment.

As I observed children working diligently both for self-satisfaction and a desire to please me, their teacher, I noticed the awakening of an inner strength emanating from many of my students. Was this the children's "spiritual embryo" that Maria Montessori often wrote about?

In 1978 my son Benjamin was born, followed closely by Jonah and Hana. One question my husband and I asked ourselves was "How do we raise children who reflect our own value system?" The other question was "What kind of people do we want our own children to become?" Given that my husband is a rabbi and educator, it seemed wise to integrate Jewish life with our children's early childhood experiences. Because of this, I found myself leaving the world of Montessori for a new adventure in Jewish early childhood, although many of Montessori's beliefs stayed with me. I worked in Jewish day schools (schools that go through sixth or eighth grade) from 1986 to 2001 in both Philadelphia and Cleveland.

In these Jewish early childhood programs, I was able to comfortably focus on universal values with a Jewish twist. Kindness became *hesed* and the word for values became *middot*—Hebrew words for these universal values. One of the biggest differences I discovered while teaching in a Jewish environment was an ability to use the tool of blessings and prayers. Such blessings helped me to observe how internal feelings of gratitude can be awakened while simultaneously enhancing external spiritual moments.

I remember one day coming into school and finding rainbows dancing all over the walls of our indoor motor room. Everyone—parents, children, and educators alike—was mesmerized by the presence of the reflected lights of color. I knew there was a blessing for rainbows, but I didn't know it by heart. Being in a Jewish school meant there was always a rabbi at hand. The children and I went to find the rabbi who shared the blessing with us:

וּרמֲאַמְּב םׇיׇקְו וֹתׇיְרְּבַב ןׇמֱאֶנְו תׇיְרְּבַה רֵכוֹז םׇלוֹעׇה ךֶלֶמ וניֵהוֹלֱא 'ה הׇתׇּא ךוּרׇב

Baruch ata Ado-nai Elo-heinu melech ha'olam zocher ha'brit v'ne'eman bivrito v'kayam b'ma'amaro.

Blessed are You, Lord our God, King of the universe, who remembers the covenant, and is faithful to His covenant, and keeps His promise. (Chein 2016)

The blessing helped to enhance our moment of wonder and gratitude for this beautiful experience. We did not focus much on the words and meaning of the blessing. For now, we were more interested in marking the moment with special words.

After reciting the blessing, the children began to ask a myriad of questions: Why is there a rainbow? Why today? Where is it coming from? Can we make our own rainbows? Can we touch it? Can it come on me? The children were also interested in the variety of colors, and some children thought they could see some sequencing or order to the colors. The experience was very exciting, but rather than being loud and boisterous, we initially all stopped and caught our breath in response to all the beauty that surrounded us. The questions came in hushed voices.

By this time in my career, I had the good fortune to be working at a school that supported art education and children's inquiry. I had also spent many years studying and reading about Reggio Emilia philosophy. In Ohio, where I was living at the time, I was able to participate in Reggio Emilia study groups, attend classes at Kent State University, and participate in workshops on Reggio Emilia philosophy taking place all over the United States.

Looking back at the day the rainbows came to visit, I would say that the experience emerged from a shared spiritual moment. Back then, even in a religious school, there was no language for acknowledging this type of experience as nurturing children's spiritual development. Yes, the children and I explored many perspectives of rainbows, and we all grew in our understanding of the relationship between light and water. The children explored color mixing and color comparisons, and one little boy named Eli renamed some of the crayons in the crayon box. In retrospect, I believe this was Eli's way of connecting spirituality to the colors in the rainbow. The children also grew in their ability to interact with one another through shared discussion and research. But because we had no awareness or language to discuss the spiritual side of the experience, spiritual development appeared to have been neglected.

A Growing Need to Talk about Spiritual Development

Years later, after my own children had grown old enough to leave the Jewish day school for public high school, after I spent a year revisiting Montessori by acting as a lead Montessori educator back in Philadelphia, and after visiting Reggio Emilia, I moved into a low socioeconomic, inner-city school in Cleveland.

This is where I was hit with the big question about spiritual development. Here is how it all unfolded. While working as teacher and director at the Goodrich-Gannett Neighborhood Center (GGNC) in the heart of one of the poorest neighborhoods in Cleveland, I was also working on a book called *What's Jewish about Butterflies?* with Maxine Handelman. The book was about supporting Jewish early childhood educators who wanted to bring Jewish values into their classrooms. While I would sit writing, I would look over the sleeping children. Many came from lower-income families and had one or both parents absent from their lives. I loved them deeply and they loved me back. They were all growing and learning, and things were running smoothly. I felt great about the work I was doing, but something, some ingredient, was missing, and I simply could not put my finger on it.

I had brought in practical-life materials learned from my Montessori years to guide the children toward deep focusing, which I have come to see as a primary ingredient of spiritual development. For me, being able to focus is a like a window into one's inner self. From brain research, we learn that the ability to focus is connected to what neurologists and developmental psychologists call *executive functioning*—focus or inhibitory control, cognitive flexibility, and working memory (Semrud-Clikeman 2017). Back in 2002 I wasn't thinking about executive functioning, but I noticed that most of the children, even the big kids (those five to nine years old), would come into the classroom to have a try at the practical-life trays. Each tray held two small bowls. One bowl was filled with rice, beans, acorns, sand, or something similar. I would place a pretty container (such as a wooden box or glass vase) next to the trays to hold an assortment of spoons and tongs so the children could choose which to use. After selecting a spoon and tray, each child would carefully carry the chosen tray to a table, sit down, and beginning spooning the contents of one bowl to the other with careful deliberation.

There were also trays with small glass pitchers filled with colored water for pouring. Whether the children were spooning or pouring, there appeared to be an invisible thread connecting hand, eye, mind, and body. As the children worked on individual tasks, their faces glowed, their expressions were serious, and you could tell that they were completely engaged in the task. My observations led to a deeper understanding of how children might actually be developing a sense of self while engaging in this work or self-selected play. I definitely think something big and important was happening.

I also brought to my classroom environmental aspects inspired by the Reggio Emilia philosophy. The beauty within my classroom did not quite compare to the photographs shared by Margie Carter and Deb Curtis in

their book *Designs for Living and Learning*, but my goals were aligned to a similar vision. In other words, the room was filled with beauty, order, and materials strategically placed to stimulate ideas, discussion, questions, projects, and so on. The children were engaged and happy. So what was bothering me? What was missing?

One spring day, while in the outdoor playground, a small boy came up to me with a big grin of delight across his face. He slowly opened his hand and showed me his prize. It was a long, wet, curly worm. If you knew me well, you would know that I truly love all things from nature. I would normally be delighted to see a worm. But that day, I froze. I realized that back in my Jewish early childhood days, I would have access to a blessing. In fact, Maxine and I talked about blessings from the heart in the very book that we were writing. These are blessings that are made up to serve any specific purpose at any moment. Most Jewish blessings begin with "Blessed are you, God." For children in a public-school setting, there is no reason at all not to create a blessing from the heart to acknowledge a spiritual moment. This is when I first realized what ingredient was missing in my inner-city classroom—a lens for spiritual development. I could have responded to the child with the worm by saying, for example, "Thank you, world, for giving us amazing creatures." I could have turned to the child and asked him to share his gratitude in finding this worm. But I didn't do anything.

This lack of response led me to the Internet, where I typed in a variety of search terms to reflect spiritual development and the spirituality of young children. For spiritual development, I found very little that pertained to children. When I typed in *spirituality*, I found lots of material reflecting transcendence, God, and religion. I was left wondering what to do next.

Over the next two years, I could not vanquish my thoughts of spiritual development for young children. People told me to forget it; *spirituality* is an uncomfortable word. "You cannot bring spirituality into an early childhood classroom," they said. But it followed me wherever I went. Finally, the only option left was to do my own research.

In 2005 I enrolled as a doctoral student at Walden University, and I never looked back. Even in an academic setting, I had to fight battles to make my research a reality. With lots of hard work, a steadfast belief in what I was working on, and the help and support of my husband, Rabbi Jeffrey Schein, as well as my adviser, Dr. Amie Beckett, I made it through.

Today, I can share an ever-evolving definition of spiritual development for young children that arranges this knowledge into a system that changes how we see and use that which we know (see the following diagram). Spiritual development is as complex and invisible to the naked eye as intellectual development, as deep-seated as emotional development, and as integrative as social development. In fact, my research shows that spiritual development may, in fact, be the precursor to all other areas of development. More work needs to happen in this field. For now, I am pleased to share the language of spiritual development so that we can begin the wonderful discovery of what is actually taking place within early childhood environments throughout the United States as we use this new and exciting lens to help children gain a better beginning to life and learning.

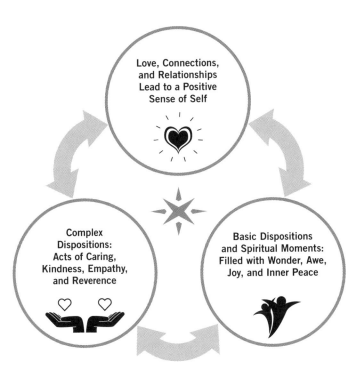

In this system, the arrows go in all directions, indicating that spiritual development can be nurtured in many ways throughout one's lifetime.

CHAPTER 1

The Developing Self

THE DEFINITION of spiritual development that emerged from my social constructivist / grounded theory study begins with love, a concept so simple, so universal that we all know and respect it as vitally important for healthy human development.

When the word *love* is used at the beginning of life, it is in reference to the love a parent feels for a child. Such a definition of love connotes affection, adoration, and devotion. It is an unconditional kind of love that initiates a trusting relationship between parent and child. To conduct my own research, I interviewed people about spiritual development. Throughout this book, I have included quotes that come directly from those interviews. Here is what one study participant says about love in relationship to spiritual development as it emerges at the beginning of one's life:

When we are born to this world, trust is the most basic mental, physical, spiritual need, because [infants] are so dependent. *Is someone going to take care of me? Love me?* Of course, they aren't thinking these things, but they learn to trust based on whether their needs are taken care of, whether they are cuddled and loved. It is trust that makes one feel safe and secure. It is trust that brings contentment. It is trust that gives us a sense of our own self-worth and allows us to value those around us. Love and acceptance, care and concern, tenderness and contentment all support the developing personhood of the infant.

This participant speaks of trust as it develops out of the love a parent bestows on an infant. The love that guides parents to act with a sense of responsibility and respect initiates feelings of trust within the infant. Many theories support such ideas, each offering their own unique perspective to the topics of love, relationships, and the development of a child's self-awareness. We will look at some of those theories in this chapter that were introduced by people such as Pestalozzi, Bronfenbrenner, Bowlby and Ainsworth, Montessori, and Buber, some of whom were born over a century ago. Thanks to current brain research and neuroscience, we now know there is scientific evidence to support these ideas.

Research on Love and Connections

PESTALOZZI

Johann Heinrich Pestalozzi was a Swiss educator who lived from 1746 to 1847. I bring Pestalozzi to this discussion because of what he had to say about the relationship between mother and child. Pestalozzi wrote that children who are loved and whose spirits are nurtured are capable of an amazing human response—they love back! The power of this statement is

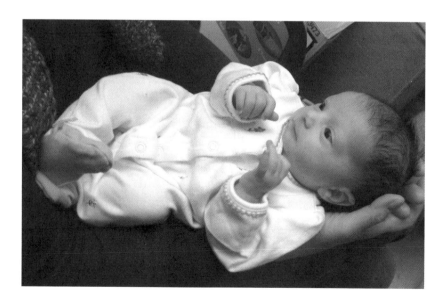

deeply important. Pestalozzi is saying that sophisticated emotional qualities such as empathy, understanding, or compassion are not taught but emerge from the child depending on how one is treated and loved at the beginning of life. I have personally witnessed infants' displays of these sophisticated responses. Right after an infant has been fed and is gently being patted on the back, the child will respond by returning the pat. Such moments are indeed precious and telling of an infant's capacities of loving back.

Using broad strokes, Pestalozzi's theory of educational philosophy can be described as "four spheres" of relationships. The first sphere is about human relationships. Children learn about human relationships at home when their parents or other family members help to create bonds of love. The second sphere, as described by Pestalozzi, focuses on a connection between the way an individual is valued and the level of self-determination or initiative that is evoked by the relationship or connection. In other words, desire and will can be triggered by relationships. If a child is loved and loves someone in return, the child will develop and use inner desire, will, and determination to please that person, as well as themselves. The third sphere describes a child's ability to move beyond the parent-child relationship into a deeper understanding of self, revealed through the child's developing character, attitudes toward learning, and a sense of duty or responsibility. This is where cultural values, the idea of consequences, and moral development become apparent. For a child to move into this realm, the child must first develop a sense of who she is: a love of self that develops alongside the child's relationships to all that lies beyond and around herself. The final realm includes a more sophisticated inner ability and desire to do what is right and good, no longer just for oneself but for others. In this last scenario, the child has grown into a human being who has internalized what is expected of her to live in her given society and culture. This sequence of development is ultimately intended to bring to the child feelings of peace and belonging. Children who have opportunities to be loved and nurtured in this way have a greater chance of growing into adults who can then bestow unconditional love on their own children. Ultimately, love provides a needed quality for human wellness and well-being.

BRONFENBRENNER

Urie Bronfenbrenner, a Russian-born American psychologist, built a theory of development that places the child in the center of concentric circles that grow ever more complex as the child's human relationships extend from family to school and neighborhood to community and beyond. Though Bronfenbrenner's theory is similar in construct to Pestalozzi's in that Bronfenbrenner (1973, xvii) believed that all "children need people in order to become human," his ultimate conclusions about children living in the United States during the mid- and late twentieth century were not so positive.

While working with a grant from the National Science Foundation, Bronfenbrenner began to see how "models, peers, and group forces" provide powerful influence upon the developing child (v). Some of this work took place as Bronfenbrenner researched and analyzed two worlds of childhood—the United States and Russia (then known as the USSR). He discovered that child-rearing practices of very young children in the USSR focused on a concept of *vospitanie*, meaning the development of the child's "qualities as a person—his values, motives, and patterns of social response" (xxiv), a concept that does not translate easily to our English language. To develop this quality of *vospitanie* in Soviet children, caregivers were asked to keep children warm and safe through loving and tender ways, while simultaneously emphasizing "obedience (*polushanie*) and self-discipline (*distsiplinirovannost*)" (9). Soviet children were viewed as bringing joy to family and society, and their caregivers were called "upbringers" and were well respected (17).

After *Two Worlds of Childhood: U.S. and U.S.S.R.* was first published in 1970, Bronfenbrenner was invited to the White House Conference on Children held in December of that year. At this conference, he reported that "America's families, and their children, are in trouble, trouble so deep and pervasive as to threaten the future of our nation" (Bronfenbrenner 1971, 252). The reason behind this threat was parental neglect of the United States' children. At the time of this report, the United States stood "thirteenth among the nations in combating infant mortality," and violence of children was on the rise (252). Bronfenbrenner believed that scientific research and human experiences have shown that children need to be loved and connected to caring adults to become fully human and to reach their own potential. Again, the topic of love reigns as significant.

Research on Love and Attachment

BOWLBY AND AINSWORTH

This brings me to what most early childhood educators and parents within the United States already know, or should know, about love: love and attachment are requirements for healthy development.

John Bowlby, a developmental psychologist, was inspired by Konrad Lorenz's work on imprinting behaviors of baby geese. Lorenz's work with geese led him to discover that all baby goslings follow and learn from the first moving body they see after birth. Bowlby wondered if something similar to imprinting might exist for human infants. This question led him to his research that determines that infants and young children "should experience a warm, intimate, and continuous relationship" with one's mother or significant caregiver. Within this relationship, both adult and child should experience "satisfaction and enjoyment" (Bowlby 1951, 13). It is important to note here that both adult and child play significant roles in this relationship.

Later, Bowlby partnered with Mary Dinsmore Ainsworth who was researching attachment between children and mothers in Uganda. Ainsworth ultimately provided Bowlby with the necessary empirical evidence to support his theory. Together, Bowlby and Ainsworth constructed a theory of love and attachment, demonstrating to the world that positive attachment has a significant and meaningful role in children's personality development. In the end, both Bowlby and Ainsworth believed that positive love and attachment, based on mutual respect between child and adult, would guide children to develop positive self-worth and instill in them a desire and need to explore their environment (Bretherton 1992).

Today, the theory of attachment remains important and relevant, as reflected in a relational-based approach to child rearing (Wittmer and Petersen 2014). Feeling safe and secure has taken precedence over feelings of love and attachment. Vygotsky (1962) reminds us that language can determine one's thoughts. In my opinion, a focus away from love and attachment has created a significant impact on child-rearing practices in the United States. *Safe and secure* has been defined in ways that negate or push aside the value of love needed at birth for healthy human development and well-being.

For some children, *safe and secure* translates to being overly protected, coddled, pampered, and watched. These children live in a world in which they are told not to touch, climb, or play for fear they may hurt themselves, get sick, or worse. This is where the metaphor of the helicopter parent was born. *Helicopter parent* refers to parents who are overprotective and show too much involvement in the lives of their children. Children being raised by helicopter parents often lack resilience and competencies needed to become fully functioning adults.

In other homes you might find a different scenario, but one just as worrisome: children who are safe and secure but have caregivers without time for loving relationships. Children who find themselves in the foster care system or whose parents are stressed and overworked may not be receiving the kind of love or attention they need to flourish. In either case, too much attention or too little can produce children who may be physically safe but not feeling loved, seen, or respected—and therefore, not spiritually nurtured in a way that helps them reach their full human potential.

I can't help but think that it is here that the gap in learning begins. The reality is that it only takes one person to bestow this kind of love on a child. It has been my experience that when children do develop strong love and attachment, they are observably ready to look beyond themselves into a world that is open to new possibilities. These children are more than ready to participate in new and exciting learning experiences. They often possess deep desires and abilities to explore their environments, to seek out knowledge, and to know how to build a number of new relationships. But before a child can develop any shared relationships, she first needs to develop a strong and clear sense of who she is—a personal sense of self.

Spiritual Development in Action

AT THE AIRPORT

One day at the airport I saw a very small child looking all around. To me it seemed as if she was trying to get someone, anyone, to notice her. It reminded me of my visits to inner-city schools back in the '90s and the early part of 2000. I would walk into a classroom and the children would swarm around me, seeking out closeness, attention, and hugs and affection from me, a perfect stranger. As I watched the young child at the airport, I realized that this child and my past experiences were examples of children being resilient. Children know what they need, and they find many ways to get the love and recognition they require for further learning to occur. It is we, the adults in a child's life, who need to read the cues so we might support children where they are. It is up to us to help children develop a sense of who they are. Luckily, the very young child in the airport was finally able to get her mother's attention. This baby was one of the lucky ones. Her mother made raspberry sounds, blew air bubbles, and chatted in a language I did not know or understand. These words for this three-month-old child were just what she was asking for. Mom was seeing her child and offering her recognition and spiritual nurturing. The child responded in turn, and I witnessed a lovely dance between the two of them.

Research on Developing a Sense of Self

In 1896, Maria Montessori became the first female Italian doctor of medicine. Upon graduation, she began working with children whom others deemed uneducable. Facing this challenging task, she made some remarkable discoveries about how children learn.

Montessori borrowed the idea of stage development from her colleague Jean Piaget. Stage development implies that one step leads to another and that each step must be fully developed before moving to the next sequential step. Piaget's and Erikson's theories of development are both good examples of stage theory development.

Just like Pestalozzi and Bronfenbrenner, Montessori (1967, 84) came to believe that love was also a key ingredient for healthy human development. She describes the first stages of a child's development as a time in which love is both needed and bestowed on the child. Montessori suggests that in the best scenario, the child is born out of love, into love, and grows "in love with the world." Montessori believed that "the love we find in infancy shows what kind of love should reign ideally in the grown-up world" (31). Equally important is Montessori's belief that deep love for a child is capable of awakening the child's "spiritual embryo."

Metaphors for Describing Spirituality

THE SPIRITUAL EMBRYO

In a book edited by Stuart M. Matlins, Arthur Green (2001, 5) describes three words used to help us understand Montessori's phrase *spiritual embryo*. These words, transliterated from Hebrew, are *neshamah* (soul), *ruach* (spirit), and *nefesh* (breath). *Nefesh* represents the "essence of the person" and is the Hebrew word for *breath*. The idea of breath as spirit is a universal concept. The word *nefesh* describes the physical side of spirituality, and *ruach* represents a person's uniqueness. For me, these words signify our human ability to think, reason, and remember as well as to be spiritual. Together, they describe our internal life force.

Whether one believes in God or not, it is still possible to acknowledge the existence of a life force that moves us forward. Montessori (1963, 15) described this life force as "the miracle of creation from nothing," the unconscious growth and development of "a new creature born (often out of love) into the world." Montessori saw this new creature not merely as a material body but as also containing a vital force. This vital force is synonymous with the metaphor of spiritual embryo. My participants and I found the concept of spiritual embryo descriptive and important for our discussion of spiritual development of young children. We also appreciated Montessori's metaphor of children's absorbent minds.

THE ABSORBENT MIND

The absorbent mind refers to children's exceptional ability to learn culture, language, and nuances unknowingly and continuously from one's environment (Montessori 1967). Together, these two metaphors—spiritual embryo and absorbent mind—help to describe how a child might begin to know oneself, all beginning with love.

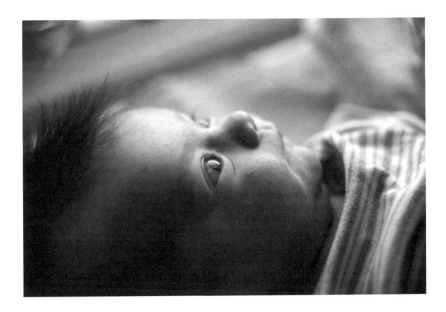

Montessori came to these understandings using multiple perspectives. They include her deeply ingrained scientific framework; her own personal Christian upbringing; Freud's idea of unconsciousness, which had just been published and was becoming quite popular; and finally, the invention of the microscope, which allowed the human eye to see what had been invisible to the naked eye. I believe it is possible for all these ideas to merge together to produce a new theory built on Montessori's concepts of spiritual embryo and absorbent mind. It looks like this:

As the spiritual embryo is ignited by external gifts of love, the system begins to push forward. The spiritual embryo is a driving force that ignites the child's absorbent mind, which then helps the child to develop loving relationships. The child's absorbent mind reflects an infant's mental, social, and emotional capacity to engage and connect to the outside world, including the child's ability to respond and learn from the touch and loving look of the person who is caring for him. This kind of self-awareness opens up each human being in such a way that invites the development of new and lasting relationships.

Other Supporting Theories

It is curious to note that most of the theorists written about in this chapter wrote their theories long before current brain research. Yet the brain research of today continually validates that children require love, attachment, and touch to support and sustain healthy brain development (Raikes and Edwards 2009).

The research of Bowlby and Ainsworth on love and attachment has already been discussed. Bowlby suggests that "intimate attachments to others are the hub around which a person's life revolves, not only as an infant or a toddler but through adolescence and the years of maturity and into old age" (quoted in Honig 2002, 19).

MENTAL MODELS

Mental models are an individual's deeply ingrained assumptions, generalizations, pictures, or images that consciously or unconsciously direct that person's understandings, actions, and behaviors (Senge 1990). One's happiness or well-being can actually affect one's mental models. Nel Noddings (2007), known for her theory on happiness, emphasizes that attachments, which she calls connections, promote happiness, and she believes that happiness should be included as one of the primary goals of education. Her position does not negate the importance of struggle and conflict in learning, as reflected in the term *provocation* in Reggio Emilia philosophy or in Erikson's stage of trust versus mistrust. It is instead an acknowledgment that happy people are better learners; rarely mean, violent, or cruel; and better able to deal with the adversities that are a part of life. Noddings defines happy people as those whose needs are satisfied, but she differentiates between (a) needs and wants and (b) the need for positive personal and public relationships. Cooper and Brna (2002) document similar findings indicating that friendship, comfort, and collaboration have a positive effect on children's learning and engagement. Wilson and Schein (2017) speak about the importance of being welcoming, listening, and caring. For this discussion on young children and spirituality, happiness is built on friendship, comfort, and collaboration, which affect the "development of character, spirit, intellect, and personality" (Noddings 2007, 4–5). In general, neurologists and brain researchers are suggesting that relationships and deep connections are very important for a child's well-being.

Bowlby also referenced the concept of mental models. More specifically, Bowlby explained in his three-volume series on attachment that all humans develop an internal working model of the self and an internal working model of others. The self-model and other-model are built off of early experiences with an infant's primary caregiver. These models help to shape an individual's expectation of future interactions with others and interactions within interpersonal relationships. In other words, this self-model will determine how the individual sees herself, which will impact self-confidence, self-esteem, and dependency on others. The modeling that is done in relationship to others will determine how an individual sees others, which will impact her avoidance or approach orientation, loneliness, isolation, and social interactions.

Developing a Sense of Self

I believe that this is where and how children truly find their own sense of self: through the eyes of the person who is bestowing love on them. This is the same love that awakens an infant's spiritual embryo. As the infant stares out into the world, what he sees is a reflection of self through the loving eyes of a parent or caregiver. The child's absorbent mind is able to take this all in, every nuance, every glance. In fact, research tells us that infants and young children are wired to learn (Lally, Mangione, and Greenwald 2006; Shonkoff and Phillips 2000). The infant sees loving eyes looking at something that the infant does not yet know—oneself. This is where one's concept of self is born and when one's individual essence is felt with some recognition. Unfortunately, at this time, there is no way to tell how consciously aware an infant might be of this moment. Nevertheless, to the trained eye, something magnificent occurs when an infant's glance meets the eyes of a person who is recognizable and loving.

This moment is what I like to call "the baby love stare." This stare is so focused, so intense that someone could walk between the baby and her caregiver and she would be able to maintain her intense focus. It is strong and

impenetrable. I see this baby love stare as the making of the love bond that Pestalozzi, Bronfenbrenner, Bowlby and Ainsworth, and others speak of. It is a stare that is common in infants who are receiving love and are growing in their own capacity to relate to another. Through this process, an infant's self is born.

Without love and attachment, the process of knowing oneself is a much more difficult and bumpy process. However one gets there, the next step for spiritual development for all children, once the self is known, is the development of deep connections and the evolution of other important relationships. Once there is a self, there can be connections and relationships.

Research on Building Relationships

BUBER'S "I AND THOU"

Martin Buber, an Austrian-born Israeli Jewish philosopher, looked at development through the lens of the individual in relationship to others. He uses the term *I and thou*. The word *thou* is best interpreted by referring to the German adjective *offenburg*, which transforms the meaning of *thou* to mean "you-spirit" in a way that holds no religious connotation (Buber [1923] 1996, 57). It implies breath. Buber then defines spirit as existing between I and thou, as if it were the air we breathe (Buber [1923] 1996). Spirit is therefore also synonymous to the breath within each of us. This is a rather commonly held belief by other cultures throughout the world.

This is yet another point where love and spirit come together. When a child receives love, both giver and receiver are seen through loving eyes, and both are being nurtured spiritually. The infant uses a sense of self while the giver of love becomes aware or reacquainted with the wonder and miracle of life and development that is looking back at him. This scenario might be defined by Buber as an I-Thou relationship as opposed to an I-It relationship.

Buber's theory can also be applied to the spiritual interchange between infants' predispositions to seek out something larger than themselves and their need to develop relationships with individuals, groups, and the environment. In fact, very young children are capable of forming I-Thou relationships with just about anything. These relationships touch on all developmental domains of learning, including but not exclusive of spiritual, cognitive, social, emotional, and physical development.

These ideas were reinforced by participants in my research study. One participant shared that once a child receives love, develops attachment, and has a developing sense of self, then the child is able to look outward.

In Buber's terms, this means that an I-It becomes an I-Thou, which means that a child can have a very important relationship with an inanimate object. The following is a story of an infant having I-Thou moments with an object—in this case, a large colorful rattle that produces sound.

Here is what happened. The adult in the room snatched away a piece of tissue the baby had been playing with. Naturally, the baby started cry-ing—not just a little cry, but a big wet cry. The educator did nothing to soothe the child, so I leaned over and quietly suggested she might try to find something that this baby loves that might help him to stop crying. She found a big yellow-and-orange plastic rattle. She placed it within arm's reach of the child. He took it and within seconds was exploring his new toy. First, he looked at it. Then he gave it a little shake followed by a longer shake. Soon he was shaking that rattle and looking all around, as if to say, "Hey, look what I have. Isn't it cool? Do you like it too?" The joy on his face was completely opposite from the tears of a few minutes earlier.

The toy originally was an *it*, an object; yet this baby related to the object with his entire being and using all his senses. When this occurs, which is often for most babies and young children, the object becomes a *thou*, a close friend, thus creating an important relationship. The baby explored the *thou* object in the immediate moment with a complete wholeness of self. In the end, the *thou* becomes more than an *it* could ever be. Moreover, for Buber ([1923] 1996, 60) such experiences can be viewed as the "cradle of actual life." Buber goes on to say, "Such work is creation, inventing is finding. Forming is discovery" (61). From an educational perspective, discovery is a form of learning similar to Dewey's theory of children's acquisition of knowledge through their experiences and use of senses.

A similar scenario occurs as children experience spiritual growth and development. "I/Thou relationships are completely reciprocal in the same way as love is reciprocal" (Leutenberg and Schein 2017). These words once again conjure up the image of an infant patting the back of a caregiver after

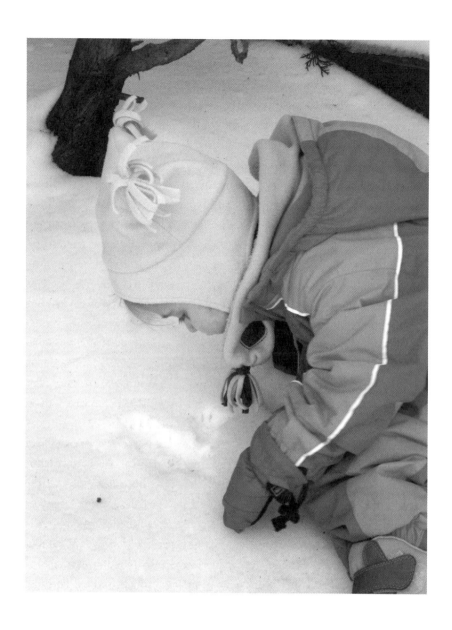

having been fed. Other examples might originate from adult experiences in watching a child experience a first achievement, such as taking a first step, seeing a first snowfall, or eating a first spoonful of solid food.

In such instances, the adult's presence and response enhance the infant's experience through language, facial and body expressions, excitement, encouragement, and simply by sharing in the moment. The child, unknowing but equally important to the relations, is also reciprocating a feeling of spirituality to the adult by reminding the adult of the importance of

newness, wonder, and the joy of new experiences. Together, child and adult share in I-Thou moments that both strengthen the love bond between them as well as stimulate each individual's spiritual embryo (Leutenberg and Schein 2017).

MORE ABOUT RELATIONSHIPS

Once children begin to develop relationships—whether described as I-Thou relationships, friendships, I-It relationships, or a stronger relationship with oneself—there are several additional perspectives that can support their spiritual development. Self-awareness, for instance, may be a more helpful concept than self-esteem. A child's ability to be open, receptive, creative, imaginative, and mindful is also important. Finally, it is sometimes necessary for adults to think about when and how to offer praise to children so that it is productive and helpful.

A New Way of Looking at Self-Awareness

During my research, I discovered that self-awareness differs greatly from a child's development of self-esteem. Self-awareness focuses on helping children learn about themselves in relationship to all that exists around them. Self-awareness can lead children toward development of healthy relationships that continue to multiply with age and experience.

Focusing on developing children's self-esteem can often feed the ego and fail to help children know themselves—both their strengths and their weaknesses. The overarching goal of helping children develop self-awareness is not just about helping children feel good about themselves but about helping children develop an honest view of themselves while also supporting their ability to grow, develop, and connect with others. If children know what they are good at, they can in turn offer help and support to others. If they realize what they need help, growth, and support in, they can learn to seek it out. Both scenarios support the child's self-awareness and also help to strengthen the child's ability to relate to others.

One participant in my study shared that, for her, spirituality is about heart-to-heart and heart-to-mind connections. She describes how human

beings connect on a very primitive level and that this special connection often happens when one human being is helping others. She also mentions a child's deep connection with the earth. For this relationship, she suggests that children can just focus on six square inches of their front lawn. I would add that children can make connections with nature simply by looking out of a window at trees, grass, or waterways.

Self-esteem has a tendency to get lost in these descriptions, but self-awareness does not. This is why I caution the use of *self-esteem* while encouraging the language of *self-awareness*. Focusing on self-awareness can take both educator and children to amazing places, while focusing on self-esteem runs the risk of stopping with each child.

The differences between self-awareness and self-esteem may be confusing, but clarity emerges when one stops to analyze the differences from the perspective of spiritual development. Self-awareness, unlike self-esteem, places the child into a social setting that involves connection to family, friends, culture, and community. Self-esteem, on the other hand, is about filling a child's ego up as if it were a balloon. Instead of helium or air, the child is being filled up with too much sense of one's self. Too much sense of self can lead to an inflated ego.

But children, we have learned, are not at all egocentric by nature. Rather, it is society's perception of infants as being egocentric that has created these misconceptions. Freud and Piaget, in different ways, popularized the idea that young children are egocentric. In discussing self-awareness, the key word is *balance*—balance between self and others with a focus on respectful relationships.

If we think of infants as learning about themselves and their relationship to the world, none of their actions seem egocentric at all; rather, we see infants as constructing knowledge of themselves and the world. Therefore, our vision of children and our reactions to their behaviors greatly determine how we view these qualities.

If self-esteem is about filling up a child's ego like a balloon, then we can also talk about the idea of the child being filled up with so much "self" that the balloon could burst. There is no risk of this happening with self-awareness. The more self-awareness a child acquires, the more worldly and knowledgeable he becomes of himself and of all that lives around him.

Taking Another Look at Praise

Inappropriate and excessive praise can actually create disharmony for young children. It can prevent children from seeing a more accurate reality on which they can build their own personal belief system. The excessive use of praise can also send an indirect message to children that the affirmations may hold some contradiction, actually indicating that they are not worthy of the praise at all. This happens when a child is praised for something she personally does not believe to be true or which is absolutely not true. An example of this might be a child who is told she is the best artist in the world, yet she either knows or perceives she is not. One of two things can happen: either she develops an inflated ego or a deflated one. In both cases, deep connections and healthy relationships are thwarted and a child's sense of self is skewed. This child's reality of self becomes blurred, and an authentic sense of self-awareness is difficult to envision.

Dr. Sylvia Rimm, psychologist and parenting specialist, agrees that too much praise is harmful to children. She coined the term *throned child*. This is a child who is constantly praised, thinks very highly of himself and little of others, and because of this has an inflated ego. As an early educator, I have seen many such children. They often enter a classroom expecting all eyes to be on them, and when this does not occur, negative behavior ensues. Temper tantrums, meanness, and other attention-getting tactics are often used by these children in an attempt to get the attention they have learned to crave. They need attention so badly that they are happy to receive any kind of attention, including negative attention. According to Dr. Rimm (2008), building a child's self-esteem with too much praise can lead to feelings of insecurity and pressure.

Today, educators and researchers believe that praise should be meaningful and authentic. Again, the goal is to develop children who have healthy self-awareness and an ability to form positive relationships with others. Appropriate and proper praise requires parents and educators to closely and purposefully observe children to glean an understanding of each child's disposition. The important thing to remember is that appropriate praise can help to build a child's self-awareness whereas inappropriate praise can lead to distorted self-esteem.

Conclusion: Nurturing Children's Sense of Self

Knowing a child's disposition provides important insight for parents and educators as the child begins to look outward into the world. Adults begin to ask themselves about the kind of experiences they might make available to the child they are observing. Each child seems to come into the world with distinct preferences, passions, and simple likes and dislikes.

The concept of disposition will be looked at more closely later in this book. Although each child has a unique disposition, many developmental similarities also exist between all children. One of the hypotheses of my doctoral research study was the belief that all domains of development are somehow affected or connected to spiritual development. The next chapter will look at developmental domains in relationship to spiritual development.

THINGS TO DO TO DEVELOP LOVE, ATTACHMENT, AND A SENSE OF SELF IN INFANTS AND YOUNG CHILDREN

☼ Accept and love the children no matter what their moods are and no matter what your mood is.

☼ Appropriately acknowledge new accomplishments. When children truly accomplish something that is praiseworthy, such as rolling over for the first time or learning to tie their shoes, share in their accomplishments by sharing in their joy.

☼ Be aware of your body language as well as the child's body language. If you say you are glad to see the child, show it with your face, your body, your words, and so on.

☼ Be patient when the child is crying. Be calm and reassure the child that it is okay to cry. On the other hand, be sure the child understands that crying can stop if the child wills it to stop.

☼ Children need structure and consistency to feel secure. Don't be afraid to have a daily routine and then occasionally create a shift or change to help a young child notice the difference.

☼ Encourage the formation of all kinds of relationships—between children and objects, children and nature, children and children, children and other educators, and with their friends and family members. Remember, your classroom is a community.

☼ Look carefully for each child's disposition and honor it without trying to change it.

☼ Say what you mean and stick to it. Be consistent so the child can learn to trust what you say.

☼ Don't forget to use the word *no*, and remember that when it is used appropriately it can also say, "I really care about you."

☼ Think of every possible way to help the children know they are loved.

☼ Think of how you can develop self-awareness instead of self-esteem.

☼ Use the infants' names so they will identify with them. They will learn that you know who they are.

☼ When nonverbal cues tell you that a child feels unhappy, model compassion. When a child expresses joy, share in the moment.

CHAPTER 2

Spiritual Development in Relationship to Other Developmental Domains

WHILE WORKING ON my dissertation, family, friends, and colleagues often asked, "Why not address the concept of spiritual development simply as part of a person's social and emotional development?" They thought this would be easier for most people to accept. They expressed fear that I might be opening a can of worms just by introducing the term *spiritual development*. In my own research, some participants initially had a difficult time answering my questions because the language of spiritual development was so new to them and sometimes uncomfortable to use. But because of all these provocations, I felt an even greater desire to stick with the term *spiritual development* along with my belief that both the concept and the language were important.

I begin this chapter with some basic assumptions and brief definitions of quality early childhood education and wholeness. Then I share perceptions from early childhood educators about spiritual development in relationship to other well-known developmental domains (cognitive, social, emotional, and physical). In the last section, I share a true story that describes the bridge between spiritual development and learning by looking at spiritual development using the acronyms STEM, STEAM, and STREAMS. Ultimately, I make the claim that while spiritual development can be considered its own domain, it can also have a significant effect on all other domains of development and learning.

Some Basic Assumptions about Spiritual Development and Young Children

Following is a list of assumptions about the spiritual development of young children that may be consciously or unconsciously shared by parents and educators:

☼ Spirituality is inborn.

☼ Spirituality must be nurtured to flourish.

☼ Spirituality is an important component for quality early childhood education.

☼ Spirituality is required to develop the whole child.

☼ Nurturing spiritual development can lead to a better society.

The first two assumptions—that spirituality is inborn and must be nurtured to flourish—were touched on in chapter 1. They are often associated with a child's spiritual embryo and an infant's intrinsic need for love and attachment.

I will address the third and fourth assumptions in this chapter along with early childhood educators' views of existing relationships between spiritual development and other domains of development. The final assumption reflects the hopes of creating a better beginning for children by introducing early childhood educators to the concept of spiritual development. One reason for writing this book is a belief that the world could be a better place if we would take time to grow, respect and understand each other, and nurture the spiritual development of each of us individually and collectively.

Quality Early Childhood Education and Wholeness

These two words, *quality* and *wholeness*, are often thrown around in early childhood education, but what do they actually mean? *Quality* is synonymous with "visions of excellence" as promoted by the National Association for the Education of Young Children (NAEYC) (Copple and Bredekamp 2009, viii) and includes safety and appropriate curriculum for young children. Such curriculum is described as developmentally appropriate for each age group of children and for each individual child. In spiritual terms, this would be parallel to seeing each child's disposition. It also requires a constant eye on health, nutrition, and the social well-being of all children, as well as cultural respect and openness toward diversity. Again, the word *disposition* comes to mind, as do concepts of respect, love, relationships, and connectedness that speak to the spiritual side of one's humanness. This ultimately means that each child and her family is truly seen and respected. Furthermore, in order to create quality early childhood settings, all early childhood educators must be trained and knowledgeable so they may provide all of the above for all children and their families.

These qualities of wholeness are equally visible within spiritual development and quality early childhood settings. Therefore, it seems that the two may actually be synonymous. Spiritual development and quality early childhood education might be one and the same without anyone realizing it.

WHOLENESS AND HOLISTIC

The word *whole*, used as an adjective, refers to a sense of completeness where parts are not "divided or disjoined." The word *whole* transforms into the word *holistic* when one is speaking about "the whole body or person," which is inclusive of body, spirit, and mind. *Holistic* is a word that speaks to a gap in early childhood education in that the concept of spiritual development is rarely referenced as a developmental domain or in relationship to other developmental domains. It is my belief, one that is shared by many others, that for early childhood education to be whole or holistic, it must be inclusive of spiritual development (Kirmani and Kirmani 2009; Harris 2007; Surr 2011). It is also my belief that quality early childhood education must include a definition, a language, a reference, and a vision of spiritual development if it is to call itself whole or holistic. This also means that quality early childhood education programs must view teaching about spiritual development as a developmental domain and as part of professional development.

All children have a right to a whole and holistic education, as do the teachers who educate them. The next question to be examined has to do with how and where spiritual development fits within the existing structure of what is known as *development*.

Spiritual Development and Other Domains of Development

In my research study, I purposefully asked participants to share their personal thoughts about any relationship they perceived between spiritual development and other developmental domains, specifically cognitive, social, emotional, and physical. I also asked them if there were any major differences between spiritual development and these other developmental domains. Their answers spoke volumes to me as I began an exploration of how and where to fit the concept of spiritual development into our American context of early childhood education.

SPIRITUAL, SOCIAL, AND EMOTIONAL DEVELOPMENT

This first quote describes one early childhood educator's thoughts on what occurs when social, emotional, and spiritual development combine to create in the child an ability to move beyond the sometimes perceived egocentrism associated with young children.

> When we speak of social-emotional development, we might think more about friendships. But when we add that spiritual moment to it, I think it takes the child more outside of [herself]. The formation of friendship can be focused on development of self. I need a friend; I need a friend to do things with; [or] I think that person should like me. But I think that the spiritual development part of it would take the child further and maybe beyond caring in terms of a sense of self. [A] sense of trust expands what we usually think of as social-emotional development.

Another early childhood educator, viewing children through the lens of social development, agreed that a special quality exists within the social relationships of children: "Some children have such strong friendships with others. There is something more that adheres the relationship, solidifies it. It goes beyond the realm of social development."

These special qualities can be seen in pictures and documentation when children greet one another. Such moments invite friendship that develops and strengthens relationships. I remember reading one such documentation on early friendship during a consultation at the Jewish Community Center in Pittsburgh, Pennsylvania. It had a series of photographs that illustrated the scope of social and emotional development as it interplayed with spiritual development in the lives of young children. The educators titled this documentation *Friendship*, and they wrote the following: "On one of our walks, we glimpsed two children reaching out to one another, which caused us to wonder how nonverbal children develop friendships. These specific photographs illustrate how two children developed a relationship. In the first photograph, both children are in strollers sitting side by side one another. A very young boy reaches out to touch the cheek of a little girl. The second child responds by looking directly at the first child. Then, she gently touches his hand, maybe to get his attention once again. The little boy responds by making eye contact and reaching back, seeming to take her hand." The educators then wrote, "Maybe the start of friendship for nonverbal children is eye contact quickly followed by a touch."

Another early childhood educator proposed that it might be impossible for her to dissociate spiritual development from emotional development. She suggests that it may be possible for someone to have a spiritual experience without it being a social experience. But, she continues, it may not be possible to have a spiritual experience devoid of emotion. For her, there exists a perpetual connection between spirituality and emotion.

SPIRITUAL AND COGNITIVE DEVELOPMENT

Early childhood educators also discussed the connection of cognitive development to spiritual development through a child's emotional desire to know. By the age of one, a child is pointing and soon begins to ask, "What's that?"

Providing an example of integration of spiritual development, emotional development, and cognitive development, one educator said, "I think why [young children] are so interested in learning facts about what is actually happening is because they are so emotionally invested. They are so touched by the whole experience." This example points back to an earlier reflection of wholeness and holistic education.

Another educator talked about how we go about teaching children their colors. She described how it involves "the lowest part of brain development, not to mention a real lack of spiritual development or cognitive development. You reduce [learning] to a name of a particular kind of color that robs all of the other possibilities." In other words, when you reduce learning and knowing to a single color—let's say yellow—the child misses out on seeing, learning, and knowing all the different hues of yellow and all of the other dimensions of "yellowness."

Other educators reflected on the brain research that a deep connection exists between social, emotional, and cognitive development. One educator said that spiritual development and cognitive development make her think specifically about brain research. She has learned that it helps a child to learn when a child is emotionally involved or emotionally touched. Stated differently, our spiritual self guides us to want to learn and then actually helps in the learning process.

Other links were discussed between spiritual development and cognition. One educator said, "When [children] discuss what they think became of our dead fish, or their pet, these can be spiritual moments. Then they grapple with big ideas."

The idea of "big questions" also became an important part of the definition of spiritual development as reflected in upcoming chapters. Someone else mentioned that a child's spiritual development occurs when the child creates an answer that connects him or her with other scholars. This educator talked about reading an article in which a child had just made a breakthrough in math and was thrilled by the awe and wonderment in discovering a shared answer. Maybe the child thought about what it means to truly understand something and how amazing it was to connect with hundreds of other people who have also solved similar math problems. I think that in both asking and then answering the question, there is the possibility of spiritual development occurring.

Here are still more examples of early childhood educators speaking about the connection between spiritual and cognitive development. In the following comments, an early childhood educator integrated cognitive, social, emotional, and spiritual development as she described her version of how children learn:

> I believe that it is the teacher's challenge to connect spiritually with every child in the classroom—not just academically but [with] a sort of Buberian I-Thou connection—and build from there. The depth of that connection will determine the extent of the learning which will occur. This is not the transfer of knowledge of language arts, math, et cetera, but something less measurable yet most measurable.

My interpretation of this individual's last words is that the learning of young children is so complex and so deeply tied to relationship and children's experiences that we can only observe parts of what is actually occurring.

Another early childhood educator introduced the terms *disequilibrium* and *dissonance* as she discussed the integration of spiritual development with cognitive development. She said that for her, disequilibrium "does not refer to cognitive dissonance in a negative sense of a child being put in a state of confusion." Instead, she talked about disequilibrium in terms of awe, wonder, and interests. She spoke about disequilibrium as the motivator that stimulates the children's interests to learn more in terms of gaining new physical or emotional experiences or creating new connections. Using this perspective, disequilibrium can be viewed as providing an internal spiritual drive that pushes children toward learning—similar to the metaphor of spiritual embryo.

Another educator spoke about creativity in an attempt to integrate cognitive development, cognitive dissonance, and spiritual development by returning to the concept of deep connections: "A sense of connectedness [leads to] creative ideas, being mindful and in the moment."

SPIRITUAL AND PHYSICAL DEVELOPMENT

Educators also spoke about a connectedness between spiritual and physical development. Two early childhood educators described how outdoor play, physical movement, and sensorial exploration can stimulate and integrate spiritual development for a young child. The first said, "There is all that physical development we get when we explore outdoors and with that active hands-on exploration, that's where we can really touch children spiritually." The other educator said, "There is really connection there, between physical development and spiritual development. You can see it in the children's faces. They glow."

First Thoughts of Spiritual Development as a System

The realization that spiritual development connects so easily to all developmental domains was one of the first indicators that the definition of spiritual development may reference a system in which the individual parts add up to create something greater than each piece, not unlike the word *gestalt* or *wholeness*. This leaves me with a new research question or a new

assumption: Spiritual development may, in fact, be the foundation for all development. In other words, spiritual development may be the drive within each and every human individual that leads toward growth, independence, knowledge, learning, and knowing. All human beings possess this spiritual embryo or unseen force. It may be up to early childhood educators and parents to keep it alive.

Reexamining STEM and STEAM

This new assumption, that spiritual development is a foundation for all developmental domains, came into full focus when I was invited to be a keynote speaker for the Bureau of Jewish Education in Southern California. They invited me to speak about spiritual development and STEAM. Here is how the story unfolds.

HOW SPIRITUAL DEVELOPMENT INTERFACES WITH SCIENCE, TECHNOLOGY, ENGINEERING, ART, AND MATH

In November 2014, I met two lovely early childhood educators from California. They participated in a workshop I offered and were so taken by the concept of spiritual development that they invited me to speak to their colleagues the following January. I was naturally excited until I heard the topic of their conference. It was STEM—science, technology, engineering, and math. I thought long and hard about that focus and eventually decided that I had to give it a try. If I believed that spiritual development might be the foundation for all learning, then I should be able to concretely connect spiritual development to the STEM subjects.

I began with definitions. I remembered what my friend Marlene Hilkowitz, an exceptional biology teacher and expert trainer of educators, said to me on hearing my definition of spiritual development: "You know, Deb, a force never stands alone. It needs something to push against. Only then can it become a force." After some thoughtful reflection, I contemplated the possibility that it is life, love, and connections that provide the initial force on a newborn that inspires growth, learning, knowing, and connections.

My next task was transmitting my findings into a language that could speak to the concept of STEM. I discovered that STEM was a twentieth-century innovation introduced to renew focus on science, technology, engineering, and math during a time of economic uncertainty. By refocusing on STEM, educational policy makers and politicians hoped to ensure a more prosperous future by preventing other countries from surpassing our children in these areas of knowledge. By the beginning of the twenty-first century, educators from the Rhode Island School of Design (RISD) championed a new term: *STEAM*. The objectives of the STEAM movement were to transform research policy by placing art and design at the center of STEM, to encourage integration of art and design in K–12 educational curriculum, and to influence employers to hire artists and designers to drive innovation.

My reflections of STEAM include thoughts on the Hundred Languages of Children, a metaphor from Reggio Emilia educators. The metaphor of one hundred languages implies that each experience is capable of bringing a new awareness, and with it new language, to each child to be used in dialogue with others (Gandini et al. 2005). With each language comes new ideas and thoughts to be communicated. This understanding is reflective of Vygotsky's (1962) theory that language and thought are closely dependent on one another. Exposure to many "languages" learned through experiences provides children with a larger pool of ideas and thoughts to use for communicating, reflecting, and understanding both the world and themselves (Schein 2012). This includes a child's understanding of science, technology, engineering, art, and math, better known as STEAM.

When I offer workshops on the Hundred Languages of Children, I often walk educators through a visualization that helps them grasp the concept of the Hundred Languages. I do this by asking everyone to take a pretend clump of clay into their hands. Then I ask, "How does it feel? Is it warm or cold? Hard or soft? What can you do with it? Can you role it into a ball? Can you make several snakes out of it?" And so on. Participants usually have specific visions that rely on their past experiences. I ask participants to push their thumb into the invisible clay and to determine the outcome. Just about everyone can image the thumb imprinted into the clay.

Next, I offer a similar experience with wire. Again I ask participants to use their imagination: "What does it feel like? What words come to mind?" Often participants will mention that it is sharp, bendable, thin, and shiny. Each material, clay and wire, offers a different language because it has different attributes. While engaging with either the clay or wire, children develop a new relationship and new language to articulate their inner thoughts and experiences—not just for clay and wire but for other ideas and experiences as well. Through these experiences, children construct their own knowledge, known today as the constructivist theory. If they experience the Hundred Languages within a group that involves dialogue, it reflects the social-constructivist understanding of how children construct knowledge. Sharing the experience with words helps children to process and construct their understanding of the experience.

For me, these imaginary experiences demonstrate the important role language and experiences bring to spiritual development and learning as described so eloquently by Dewey ([1916] 2005). Yet there still exists ambiguity or haziness surrounding the relationships between language, learning, play, and spiritual development. One interesting personal story comes to mind that clearly reflects this ambiguity from an adult perspective. In talking about STEAM and the Hundred Languages of Children, we're really talking about the complex topic of learning. We must ponder how children learn, who helps children to learn, where learning occurs, and what is actually being taught and learned.

Spiritual Development in Action

ACADEMICS, PLAY, AND LEARNING: "NO, WE ARE NOT AN ACADEMIC SCHOOL"

In 1993 I was working as a director of an early childhood program that was connected to a school that continued through eighth grade. I would proudly tell prospective parents that our program was "not academic." This was the language of the time and reflected an attitude toward a more play-based environment. Back then, I was trying to create a less stressful, less competitive environment for learning—one where the focus of teaching not only pointed to math and reading but highlighted a curriculum that was more concerned with building relationships, creativity, and problem-solving skills.

One day, on hearing me share the term *not academic*, the head of school took me aside and said, "Deb, we are a school, and therefore academics is our business!" He was right, of course, but so was I. In fact, some of the latest literature from NAEYC states that play and instruction should not be an either/or discussion. "It is not play versus learning, but play and learning" (Snow 2016). I would add that self-active play is especially connected to learning therefore making play part of the foundation of education (Nell, Drew, and Bush 2013).

That story took place many years ago, but I was reminded of it as I was preparing for the workshop on spiritual development and STEAM. I remember thinking that we still do not have an integrated language for talking about academics, domains of development, the importance of play, and spiritual development. Our colleagues from Reggio Emilia, Italy, have resolved this conflict by inviting children to explore the possibilities that emerge from their own questions. Reggio Emilia educators create classroom environments rich with opportunity so that children might explore their world together in small groups using the Hundred Languages of Children metaphor. They also become researchers as they reflect, observe, and provide materials and experiences that enrich the children's experiences. By becoming *teacher researchers*, Reggio-inspired educators can provide academic experiences built on children's play through which learning fluidly occurs. There is rarely a need to "teach."

What does this story have to do with spiritual development and STEAM? I don't think you can teach STEAM without incorporating spiritual development. From my perspective, it is important for educators to nurture both spiritual development and STEAM simultaneously. To achieve this goal, educators and parents need to develop and refine their observation skills as they listen to children's dialogues and questions and carefully watch children's explorations. It is also important to start with a vision and an honest belief that children are competent and capable learners (Montessori 1963; Raikes and Edwards 2009; Rinaldi 2006). It helps when the children's exposure to learning is meaningful, interesting, and appropriate. When all this is in place, the role of the educator is to facilitate and guide rather than to instruct and teach. This lens also helps to resolve the conflict that arose with my head of school in the story above. When this occurs, children are engaged in learning, and educators are able to support that learning by being present and providing materials, language, time, and space while also helping children build relationships.

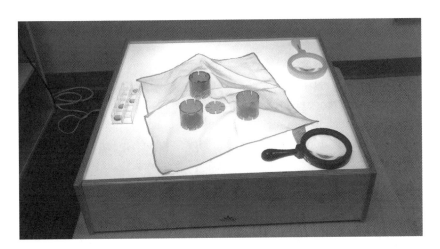

The story above also provides a resolution to the provocation that surrounds connecting spiritual development to other developmental domains. On the day of the conference where I was presenting workshops on the relationship between spiritual development and STEAM, I had an epiphany sparked by a conversation with my brother-in-law. Here is what happened.

Before the conference, I took time to visit my sister and brother-in-law. I told them about the conference and what I was planning to talk about. The next morning, my brother-in-law said to me, "Deb, why not add an *R* to STEAM and make it STREAM. The *R* could represent reading and literacy." *Wow*, I thought, *this is an amazing idea.* That same day, as I drove to the conference, I gave more thought to the newly formed STREAM acronym. For me, the word itself provided additional connections to nature and learning. Streams are beautiful and connote movement and change. A stream can easily represent lifelong learning. Steam, on the other hand is hot and wispy, and it evaporates. Furthermore, by adding the *R* for reading, I started thinking about other contributions to wholeness. *R* can represent respect, responsibility, and relationships or respect, reflection, and relationships as Wittmer and Petersen (2014) share in their book *Infant and Toddler Development and Responsive Program Planning*.

My next thought was to add an *S,* thus transforming STREAM to STREAMS. The second *S* would represent spiritual development. My friend Patti Bailie, an advocate for nature preschools, once shared with me that the *E* in STEM could stand for environment and ecology as well as engineering. When I finally took in all these changes, my mind quickly jumped to visions of STREAMS living and learning, as discussed in Curtis and Carter's revised edition of *Designs for Living and Learning*. I also thought of adding play. Now I had an acronym that read like this: STREAMS for living and learning and playing.

STEAM AND STICKS

As I prepared to speak at a conference where I would discuss with early childhood educators how to create an experience that would help them

identify, explore, and understand how spiritual development can provide the impetus for all learning, I got the idea to start collecting sticks—all kinds of sticks. They varied in size, color, shape, and density. There were short sticks, large sticks, straight sticks, curved sticks, black sticks, yellow sticks, prickly sticks, and smooth sticks, all in the hopes of representing the one hundred languages of "stickness." I carried them in my suitcase in boxes and bags.

I recruited my great-nephews in California to collect sticks for me. I wanted the educators to have a local sample of sticks to play with. I arranged the sticks on each round table so that eight to ten educators could have both an individual and a small-group experience with sticks.

Following my presentation, I realized that much learning took place and that the participants had fun and were given an opportunity to meet, talk, and work together. Relationships and connections to one another were built before any work could be accomplished. I observed that the participants were calm and showed interested involvement, and many came away with new questions about their teaching practices.

Just about everyone involved in this workshop agreed that playing with sticks can nurture one's spiritual side as well as stimulate cognition of science, technology, engineering, art, and math. This is what participants shared when they were asked to define STEAM after their experience:

S stands for *science*, meaning experimentation, comparing, observing, questioning, classifying, and hypothesizing. *T* stands for *technology*, and *E* stands for *engineering*—construction, sculptures, and designs. One table of participants wrote, "We were involved in achieving balance and stability. We used lots of problem solving to get our structures to stand." *A* stands for *art*. Participants wrote the following about art: "We focused on aesthetics, designs, pictures, diagrams, drawings, symbols, and textures." *M* stands for *math*. Participants said, "We were engaged in balancing, counting, numbering, sorting, measuring, and seriating the sticks and other natural materials."

Some groups created patterns that could also be claimed as math, technology, or art. Others created geometric figures. These last observations reflect the integration of subject matter or domains that most early childhood educators are aware of and comfortable working with. But nowhere in their written reflections did participants mention social, emotional, or spiritual development. What I was observing was the flip side of the coin. By focusing on the STEAM acronym using an academic perspective, important academic connections were made between play, natural materials, spiritual development, and learning. But the learning was mostly focused on academics, which I am fairly certain is what the conference organizers were hoping to achieve. I started to wonder what might happen if I gave a similar workshop in which I invited participants to complete the acronym STREAMS using their own ideas and thoughts.

Conclusion: Embracing STREAMS

A while back, I was given an opportunity to bring both academics and spiritual development together in a workshop I called "Spirituality, Nature, Play, and STEM: How Spiritual Development and Nature Help STEAM to become STREAMS through Play." I invited two colleagues to collaborate with me at the 2016 NAEYC conference: Robin Ploof, from Champlain College and a member of NAEYC's Play, Policy, and Practice Interest Forum, and Patty Born Selly, from Hamline University and founder of the NAEYC Nature Interest Forum. For this workshop, we provided sticks and seashells from Massachusetts, leaves from Minneapolis, and handfuls of acorns, pods, and pinecones from across the United States. The sticks and other natural materials were again arranged on a round table so that eight to ten educators could have both an individual and a small-group experience playing with natural materials.

After participants played or tinkered with the natural materials, my colleagues and I shared some of our own theories and experiences about play, nature, and spiritual development. Patty's PowerPoint showed that children have an intrinsic desire to explore, wonder, ask questions, and investigate and that nature provides a setting to do so with limitless diversity, materials, and opportunities to explore. Her PowerPoint also showed research

findings testifying that nature-based settings have been shown to have a powerful impact on children's sense of "wonder" and "connectedness" (Chawla 2012). In nature, children are inspired to reflect on their place in the world, to wonder about their connection to other beings, and to wonder about the ways of animals.

Robin interjected that play truly matters. She talked about how children are intrinsically motivated to play. She mentioned that play, learning, and development are interconnected; that children learn through the context of their play; and how play supports each of the developmental domains. Finally, she shared that play supports the development of noncognitive skills as well as providing a foundation for them.

Participants were invited to work together in small groups to define for themselves the meaning of the new STREAMS acronym. Here is what they produced:

S stood for satisfy, soothe, symmetry, special, spiritual, study, system, structure, social, senses, smell, strength, shapes, solitude, significance, and finally, spirituality and science.

T stood for texture, teamwork, transform, teacher and teaching, thing, time, touch, tinkering, transition, thinking, and trust.

R stood for reflections, responsibility, ready, read and reading, reaching, repetition, and respect.

E stood for engineering, explore and exploration, earth, energy, exercise, ecosystem, execute, experiences, environment, experimentation, energy, and engagement.

A stood for art, architecture, awakening, awareness, action, ability, acceptance, analyze, animals, and appreciation.

M stood for mathematics, movement, meditation, mindfulness, mystery, matching, meaningful, motivation, maple leaves, mother, magnitude, manipulative, maneuvers, mind-blowing, metaphysics, materials, manners, and meaning.

The final **S** was reserved for self, sensory, soothing, smile, satisfaction, surroundings, and again, science—but this time earth science and nature.

This time, participants came closer to the wholeness spiritual development strives to achieve or promises to provide. The end results of this workshop offered a glimpse into how spirituality, nature, play, and STEAM can be provided through self-active play. Again, it seems possible that spiritual development may provide a foundation on which all other domains of development can emerge, build, grow, and expand.

Things to Do to Develop a Sense of Spiritual Development as It Relates to Other Developmental Domains

☼ Always remember that children love to play, and they learn best when they are playing. Let them play—really play—without any interferences.

☼ Believe in I-Thou relationships for children and for yourself. For example, get to know an object like a seashell or a leaf really well. Make it your friend. Share it with others. Then think about how important certain people and places are to you as well. Think about all the similarities and differences that exist in the universe. For the child, this need for I-Thou moments is even more important. From these relationships come friendships and knowledge of self.

☼ Don't bother trying to teach children the names of colors; instead, go directly to hue, tone, shadow, and the like. Think big when you think of detailing the world with children.

☼ Honor children's emotions. Help children name them and let them feel the emotion before rushing them to a more comfortable or stable place. For instance, if a child is sad, ask her how it feels. If the child is too young to have language, help her by saying, "I see, you are sad. I am sorry. I wonder what made you feel sad? It doesn't feel good to be sad. Let me give you a hug."

☼ Know what assumptions you have about spiritual development. Do you believe that human beings are born with a spiritual embryo? Look at the other assumptions listed in this chapter and decide what works for you.

☼ Look for moments that pique a child's curiosity and give language to the experience. An example of this might be when you see a child looking at a shadow. Label the shadow and help the child return to it during different times of the day. These moments are not teaching moments; rather, they are sharing moments. You might say something like, "Look at the shadow we were looking at earlier." The child will notice the change, and that is all that is needed just now. To say more might interfere in the child's own observation and wonderment.

☼ Make yourself comfortable with the term *spiritual development*.

☼ Offer children one hundred ways to see the world, explore the world, and know the world. Use lots of art experiences with music, dance, movement, and artistic materials, such as paint, clay, paper, and recycled materials.

☼ Respect and honor children's verbal and nonverbal questions as reflections of both their intellectual curiosity and emotional connections to what is happening around them. This might be where brain and mind come together—mindsight.

☼ Respectfully honor a child's physical feats and development as they are part of the development of his spiritual self.

☼ Use the acronym STREAMS to provide an integration of spiritual development with social, emotional, cognitive, and physical development within your classroom curriculum.

☼ View big questions as spiritual windows into a child's way of thinking. Remember that spiritual development occurs when children ask questions and discover answers, not based on what educators or parents do.

CHAPTER 3

Curriculum, Play, and Spiritual Development

THIS CHAPTER INCLUDES language and thought for a different kind of wholeness. It is about the connection and relationship between curricula designed for young children and children's play in relationship to spiritual development. The chapter begins with a discussion of Joseph Schwab and curriculum. Schwab (1909–1988) is best known for his work in curriculum reform. He was a professor for the Education and Natural Sciences department at the State University of Chicago.

This chapter also includes other topics, such as basic and complex dispositions, imaginary play, and character development in relationship to spiritual development.

Joseph Schwab and the Four Elements of Curriculum: Teacher, Subject Matter, Student, and Milieu

While working at the State University of Chicago, Joseph Schwab wrote his famous work known as *The Practical*, a program for educational improvements based on his theory of curriculum reform.

Most educators think of curriculum as either subjects taught in an educational setting or the elements one needs to know about a particular subject. Schwab's definition of *curriculum* is broader. It includes four distinct elements: teacher, subject matter, student, and milieu. These elements are sometimes referred to as "commonplaces" and are found within most learning experiences. Together, they have been referred to as "the dance of the commonplaces" (Schein 2009, 5). I believe that spiritual development may be taking place when this dance occurs. This is to say, the spiritual development may occur when the four elements—teacher, subject matter, student, and milieu—are synchronized, integrated, and balanced in a way that meets the needs of the student who is doing the learning, each in accordance with that student's own disposition.

Let's look at each element to see how spirituality can be found within this dance of the commonplaces.

TEACHER/EDUCATOR

For young children, a teacher can be a parent, educator, grandparent, sibling, and so on. Small children can learn from anyone as long as a relationship exists between that child and the other individual. This relationship must be based on respect, honesty, and trust. This goes back to our earlier discussions of love and attachment—an important first step for both learning and spiritual development.

It is possible that the word *teacher* is not the most accurate word for this kind of spiritual guide. To be a teacher is a very lofty profession. The word *teacher* generally means to instruct or train. To be a teacher of a young child is to hold the future of the child in your hands, because the first few years of life is when the child becomes the person she will be in the future. To be an early childhood educator means to facilitate (launch or catalyze) and guide (channel or funnel) positive energy and support toward the child. This is what early childhood educators actually do. By bringing their spiritual selves to the classroom, early childhood educators use love, care, invitation, encouragement, acknowledgment, delight, and support to assist children in moving forward—learning, growing, and maturing through experiences that will sometimes touch them in profound ways. To be an early childhood teacher means that you are truly an educator or someone who mentors (guides and advises) rather than a teacher who is a trainer, coach, or instructor, although these are skills that can also be necessary and important.

As an early childhood educator, you should never simply allow something to happen. Instead, life in the classroom should be well orchestrated and highly intentional. I hear this term *allow* over and over again from early childhood educators in the United States. "I allow the children to touch the caterpillar," or "I allow them to sit wherever they choose during circle time." This is not what educators should do, nor aspire to do, because the word *allow* means to permit, consent, and tolerate. Young children require much more than to be allowed to do something. They need to be nurtured spiritually by an educator who is capable of opening up the world to each child. It is also the educator's responsibility to create new and interesting things for children to explore, which brings up the question of subject matter.

SUBJECT MATTER

The word *subject* refers to Schwab's element of learning in which the question, theme, focus, or topic being learned or studied is articulated. STREAMS for living, learning, and playing fits comfortably here (see chapter 2). But when one speaks of subject matter for young children, it is far more encompassing than STREAMS can ever be. This is because young children are learning amazing things all the time. Whether we are teaching, reading, or observing, the child is always learning.

Spiritual Development in Action

A GRADUATE STUDENT'S OBSERVATIONS OF OBSERVATION

One of my early childhood graduate students recently posted a personal reflection on infant and toddler development and curriculum. She said she had realized that it is just as important to focus on infants' routines as it is to record developmental notes. For example, "Sheila is sitting independently now" or "Jaren uses sign language for 'more' at the lunch table." She continued, saying that making notes of how much a child drinks from a bottle during a typical feeding "tells us about [a child's] development, but it is also vital information

for caregivers to share so that we can offer consistency in our care and proper [warm and caring] handling of each individual infant. Information about what a child needs in order to fall asleep, how long he typically naps, what the ambience of the room should be, et cetera, should be known by all the caregivers in an infant room, and making careful notes will ensure that everyone is updated as changes occur."

This student was referencing what is described in my research study as "getting to know a child's disposition." Knowing what a child needs to fall asleep involves developing a relationship with that child—a first step in spiritual nurturing. She was also speaking about subject matter.

Children are not usually consciously aware when learning is taking place or what is being learned. Therefore, as children construct knowledge, understanding what the child is truly learning or even doing can often be difficult. Sometimes it takes weeks or months for a concept to surface for a child or for the educator to become aware that the child has actually learned something new. But that doesn't mean that learning is not always happening; it simply means we do not and cannot always see it. Furthermore, many kinds of learning can be taking place simultaneously since young children have those amazing absorbent minds. They take in the world much better than older children or adults. The following stories help to demonstrate this.

Story of the Color Orange

As an educational consultant, I have the privilege of observing in classrooms with intentionality. One day, I came across a classroom studying the color orange. This is not my favorite topic of the curriculum because I feel that colors do not have to be taught since children are naturally exposed to them daily. In the morning, a mom might ask her two-year-old daughter, "Do you want to wear your orange top or the pink one?" Or a one-year-old boy might be asked by his big brother to bring him his blue hat. Occasionally I still see a color being explored as a classroom project. I suppose this may be necessary if and when a young child spends a good part of each day in an educational setting. If done well, an exploration of color can have a powerful impact on the children. In this case, the study turned out to have touched at least one child in a profound way.

Several weeks after the study of the color orange, I observed a child from the same class participating in a school-wide project. Amid many children from many classes, all sitting together in a large room, this little girl carefully and purposefully selected all of the orange crayons. I just happened to have been present on both these days—the day of exploration of the color orange and the day the color orange proved to be especially interesting to this little girl. As I observed her actions, I felt as if I were witnessing a spiritual moment in the life of this child. She was calm, organized, focused, and content in the moment. The integration of self and subject matter was palpable amid lots of noise.

Here is another story that highlights the ability of young children to make observations and to detect change, detail, and the nuances that occur in their daily lives.

Story of the Goose

I have a small toy goose that I have had with me during my career as an educator. I would place this goose in a visible place in my classrooms on the first day of school, usually near the door. I would watch as people came into the classroom. Almost every child would take a look at the goose. Rarely did parents take notice. Children live in the present. Buber called these *I-Thou moments*. Parents are often too busy to be in this space. Several weeks later, I would move the goose. Almost every child noticed, and some would ask, "Where's the goose?" A young crawler might look for it. But as an educator, I could miss the question on the babies' faces if I am not constantly looking for it. Educators must be watching, listening, observing, and connecting the dots of what they are seeing at all times.

Both these stories portray the power of children as learners who possess an absorbent mind. They also demonstrate how important it is for the educator to choose the subject matter with intent and purpose. The educator's work does not stop here but must continue through close observation of the child's response, interactions, and relationships to the subject matter. How else would an educator know if she had provided the right recipe for learning? Furthermore, how would the educator know what to do next?

In early childhood education in the United States, educators are often handed a curriculum. These are carefully crafted to meet the needs of all children. But the most important skills needed for an early childhood educator today are skills in listening, observing, and dialoguing with their students and other educators in order to hone their own knowledge of the children with whom they are working. Only through the use of these skills can educators determine what the children in their classrooms are ready to learn, are interested in learning, seek to know, need to know, and so on. Only then can the educator determine each child's disposition. But first the educator must get to know the child, the student who stands before her. In other words, using a goose would not work nearly as well for a child who loves cats rather than geese, nor would the color orange work for a child whose favorite color is blue. Subject matter naturally emerges through a dialogue and dance between the educator and the students that is dependent on the children's questions, interests, passions, and preferences. In order to arrive at the subject matter, educators must first develop close relationships with their students, so close that they can see to that inner spot sometimes referred to as *essence* or *soul*. This is where one finds a child's disposition and the place where spiritual development takes place.

STUDENT

So who is this student who comes to the early childhood classroom possessed with a spiritual embryo, an absorbent mind, and an inner disposition? He is a child who is just learning about his own dispositions. Each student is unique and belongs to a family. Each family lives in a community, and the school itself is a community for both child and family. It is this student that each teacher must get to know. This knowing must be a deep knowing during which the educator looks into the eyes of each child so that the child is seen in all clarity, which includes strengths, weaknesses, interests, fears, likes, and dislikes. Then the educator, together with parents or other caregivers, can help children learn about their own inner dispositions.

A Child's Disposition

The word *disposition* originated from the French word *disposicion* and the Latin word *dispositionem,* meaning order, mood, state of mind, and temperament. Our disposition relates to our likes and dislikes but goes deeper and stronger. A disposition is about strong relationships that touch us deeply. Our disposition drives us forward, possibly working in tandem with our spiritual embryo. If and when our disposition is recognized, we are in harmony with the world and our senses, and our cognitive instincts are able to turn outward to take in the many possibilities that life has to offer. In this open state of being, great learning can occur no matter what our age. This is when a child is able to look out into the world and engage with it from her own point of interest. When our dispositions are not recognized, supported, and nurtured, our sense of self or our self-awareness may be jeopardized. Nurturing one's disposition helps each of us to learn something important about ourselves. We learn about what we love. We realize our passions. We share our passions with others. We feel whole and complete (Leutenberg and Schein 2017).

Disposition Is Not the Same as Character

Please note that while the words *disposition* and *character* are often used interchangeably (Katz and Katz 2009), in the realm of spiritual development they are quite different. Disposition is something that is deeply ingrown and personal—it cannot be taught; it simply is. Character, on the other hand, is connected to a person's learned value system and the culture in which an individual lives.

There is currently a growing movement that focuses on character development in early childhood education. This is not a bad idea, as the goal is to support children's ability to learn proper behavior. What is unfortunate is that a focus on nurturing a child's disposition and spiritual development could go a lot further than an emphasis on character development. When play is added to the equation, as it was during the workshop on STREAMS for living and learning, children not only develop their character but also become aware of their own dispositions that possibly help to strengthen

These pictures show a two-year-old boy who loves cars. He uses a small car to trace a large riding car. Months later he finds, on his own, two small yellow cars in a sand and water park filled with children and lots of plastic toys. He finds the cars on two different sides of the park. After he finds the cars, he says to no one in particular, "Two cars." Then he goes off to play with his cars, again using them to explore different surfaces and areas made available to him.

their sense of self and stimulate their imagination and creativity. Again, I believe it is possible that all domains of development are touched through such experiences (Schein 2012).

Play and Children's Basic Dispositions

Play nurtures a child's basic disposition while providing access to a variety of subject matter. Following are some examples of children's play that reflect a child's basic disposition. These examples portray what happens when a person's deep-seated personal traits, or inner essence, are ignited because his disposition is met with positive external forces that produce feelings of radical amazement (Heschel 1955), often displayed as wonder, awe, joy, or inner peace (Schein 2012). Simply stated, a child's disposition needs to be matched to moments that he can deeply feel in positive spiritual ways.

Spiritual Development in Action

SMALL BOY, SMALL BLOCKS

One day I observed a young child, maybe a few months old, staring intently at some blocks. The next day, I brought out a collection of small wooden blocks for him to explore. Each block offered a unique quality—a bell in one, a mirror on the side of another, and so forth. He loved these blocks, and they were his favorite toys for quite some time (Leutenberg and Schein 2017).

This story reflects spiritual development to me because the child had clearly created an I-Thou relationship with the blocks, similar to the baby with his rattle whom we discussed earlier.

When I observe children at play, I am always reminded of how much they love and need company. An adult's presence is almost always welcomed as long as the adult is not only focused on providing instruction. Here is a story where a child simply needed someone sitting near her to make her play come alive.

Spiritual Development in Action

HAVING A FAIRY TEA PARTY

I have a friend who shared a story in which she sat on a small chair for hours while her two-and-a-half-year-old granddaughter pretended to be a fairy princess at a tea party. When her husband asked her, "What did you do all day?" she said, "I don't really know. I sat there all day while Chaya created a story and danced around and was busy and happy. All I had to do was wear a crown."

In this story, my friend created space and time for her grandchild to sow her inner disposition—one filled with imagination, creativity, and literary sophistication reflected in the details of her fantasy as she reenacted a story by heart. The child simply needed another body to make her imaginative play come to life. I have collected several such stories over time as I have watched my own grandchildren play.

Spiritual Development in Action

BAKING COOKIES

My two youngest grandchildren spend hours baking cookies together using the Montessori sandpaper letters as the cookies. (The sandpaper letters were purchased because my granddaughter seems to love tactile materials. Obviously, she also loves to bake.) Together, the two children use books as cookie sheets, a real spatula, and pretend ovens. In the midst of their imaginary play, my granddaughter once turned to me and said, "We have lots of different ovens now that our kitchen set is in the basement." "Oh," I said, "which oven are you going to use today?" "The one here under the couch," she said. She then proceeded to place the book cookie sheets, covered with sandpaper letters, under the couch. Her younger brother followed suit. He had to really focus on body control to get those cookie sheets under the couch without spilling them. Therefore, he was more invested in movement and body control, she in baking the pretend cookies.

They play like this for hours. They have the sequence down: mix the batter, lay the cookies out, bake the cookies, and let them cool. When the cookies cool, the children often collect pillows and blankets on the floor so they might take an imaginary airplane ride to visit their aunt Hana in Chicago. These children are displaying their dispositional attraction for imaginary play, something often shared by young children. While baking, they are invested in order, counting, movement, logic, and language. One can also see glimpses of the children's ability to integrate real-life events into their imaginary play, as seen in their airplane trips. My youngest grandson has flown to India because his dad's work has his dad traveling there a few times a year. But most noticeable is the children's happiness and contentment in their play. No behavior problems crop up when children are so engaged. Play that is open to the children's construction of subject matter is pure joy and delight. There, basic dispositions meet with qualities of learning that are simple and internally satisfying and yet very deep and provocative.

A side note to this story: Only recently, my youngest grandson told me he needed an oven for the outdoor toy house he had just received for his third birthday. I was reminded that each child is unique. His sister doesn't need a pretend oven to bake pretend cookies; he obviously does. When we were outside playing, I also noticed rows of rocks lined up on the children's climber. I did not need to ask who had placed the rocks just so. I knew it was my granddaughter, because ever since she could walk she has loved rocks. A child's basic dispositions are often very reliable and consistent.

Spiritual Development in Action

TRAVELING TO CLEVELAND

My oldest grandson never baked pretend cookies, although he did travel on pretend trips to Cleveland to see us, his grandparents. He played "going to Cleveland" repetitively until his entire class of two-year-olds joined him. His pretend play was always very elaborate, complete with overhead compartments for the suitcase and a turnstile to pick up the larger suitcases. This child needed no prompts at all, just his imagination and some friends. One thing I am certain of: he will never be bored (a word that should not exist in a child's vocabulary) because he has learned the skill of entertaining himself through play—another technique that helps children to make positive choices.

Stories Not Ready to Be Shared

Another observation I made is that one of my grandchildren likes to walk around mumbling at some point every day. He has displayed this behavior since he could walk. Based on my observations of him, my guess is that he is actively engaged in making up a story in which he is the protagonist. His stories are probably about sports, as sports are his true passion. I do love to see him in these moments, and I hope that they continue for a long time to come. Maybe someday he will dictate or transcribe one of his stories so others, including me, can share more directly in the story. For now, these mumblings remain private and special just for him. Maybe this reflects a private side to his disposition that I will do my best to respect.

Once again, what captures my attention most in all of this play is the joy that shines on the children's faces. As the children engage in play, their play is nurturing their spiritual development. Subjects are learned, integrated, and internalized. Different developmental domains are being challenged and stimulated. The end result is happy, healthy, whole children ready to learn and also ready to act kindly, caringly, empathetically, and with reverence.

These ways of being or ways of acting in response to the external world have been given the name *complex dispositions*. Complex dispositions are yet another aspect of the definition of spiritual development that emerged from my grounded research study. They will be explored more fully later in the book.

For now, I simply want to say that similar expressions of wonderment, awe, joy, and inner peace shine on children's faces all across the United States as they play in sand and water, paint at easels, sit quietly reading a book, or build a puzzle or block structure with good friends. There is no end to the number of ways a child's basic dispositions can be nurtured. But the environments must be made ready to meet the child's disposition so that moments of wonder are not felt by just the child but are strong enough to be made visible and shared with others. Such moments as these can be called spiritual moments.

Reflection on Imaginary Play

I currently think imaginary play is a very personal thing that reflects much of a child's basic disposition. I am intentionally using the word *currently* because this entire theory of spiritual development is still in its infant stage. This work is just one way in which an ancient topic, spirituality, is being looked at with new lenses. Because of this, I would like to see the theory remain fluid for dialogue and change as needed. So today, I think that children get to know themselves better through the process of using their imaginations. They see for themselves what they like and don't like as well as what catches their attention and what pushes them away. They practice sorting what is real from what is not and then weaving it all together again.

Ultimately, well-honed observations and listening skills help educators understand a child's dispositions, which will help determine what materials should be brought into the classroom, what questions should be asked, and what projects might be explored. In their book *From Play to Practice*, Marcia Nell, Walter Drew, and Deborah Bush (2013, 61) write that "developing the art of the play experience is, perhaps, the single most important preparation for teaching but to do this, the educator must truly know the student."

From a spiritual perspective, my colleague Jennifer Mata records in her study of kindergarten children and spirituality that imagination is one of the major attributes of spiritual development. She writes that imagination seems to support children's ability to express themselves spiritually while "relating and interacting with others" (2010, 111). She also describes how these moments are most often spontaneous and unplanned for. I am left wondering how educators find opportunities to know a child's disposition if imaginary play is not encouraged in their classrooms. Stated more strongly, if play in general is not a means for learning, how is deep, meaningful, and important learning (learning about self in relationship to life) achieved by these children?

For me, the answers to these questions are simple and yet so amazingly complex. The simple answer is that children do need play in order to learn. The complex answer asks the question, "What kind of play environment should be used to nurture the whole child?" This leads directly to a conversation about milieu, the final element required by Schwab to create the dance of the commonplaces.

MILIEU

Milieu may be Schwab's most important contribution to early childhood curriculum. Educationally, milieu refers to the environment, surroundings, and/or situations in which learning occurs (Schwab 1969). In early childhood education, one must also consider tone, color, light, space, beauty, relationships, and more (Schein 2012). Two important aspects of milieu have emerged from the grounded theory research study on the spiritual development of young children. One has been coined *spiritual moments*, and the other is about the relationship between spiritual development and nature. Both are so important that they each warrant chapters in this book.

Conclusion: Connecting Curricular Needs with Spiritual Development

Teachers should be called educators, and they too should be in touch with their own dispositions and their own attitudes and beliefs toward spiritual development. To determine subject matter, educators must hone their skills as listeners and observers so that they can discern children's dispositions. From this knowledge, educators will have a better sense of what children are curious about as they look to find what will spark the children's spiritual embryo. Naturally in doing this, educators will get to know their students; they will really see and respect the children who fill their classroom each day. Finally, milieu will be deemed important as educators think carefully about what they bring into their classrooms, how the classroom is set up, how the day flows, what the classroom feels like, and how time is spent. Milieu will be reflected on in spiritual moments in time, place, relationships, and nature, and with big questions that are capable of taking a child beyond herself. Finally, milieu must include play and imagination every day as young children continue to build who they will become by strengthening their spiritual selves.

THINGS TO DO TO CONNECT CURRICULUM AND PLAY TO SPIRITUAL DEVELOPMENT

☼ Always be on the lookout for each child's disposition. This means you must look deeply into each child. Ask yourself over and over again, "What makes this child special? What is unique? What is the child's passions?" Then provide for these qualities to flourish in the classroom.

☼ Believe in children's ability to absorb what takes place around them. To do this, you must provide a learning environment that is carefully planned and purposeful and based on solid knowledge of child development.

☼ Don't forget that spiritual development can be strengthened through one's imagination, so provide lots of space and creative materials for children to exercise their imaginations. To do this, it might be a good idea to stay clear of commercial products, because they may rob some children of initial steps in the process of using their own imaginations.

☼ Incorporate the Schwabian commonplaces of educator, student, subject, and milieu as you create lesson plans and design your classroom environment. In other words, nothing stands alone and everything is important because everything interfaces with everything else.

☼ Invite children to play and then play some more, but be sure you are near to observe what children like, question, and wonder about and also so you continue to be connected and part of a trusting relationship.

☼ Think of your work as creating a space for learning to take place within the child rather than a time to transmit knowledge from yourself to the child.

☼ Remember that the language you choose to use frames what happens; therefore, think about inviting and providing rather than allowing. Think provocation not problem. Think fluidity not stagnation. Think growth not standards. If you do all of this, so much learning will automatically take place because the spiritual embryo will be on the move.

CHAPTER 4

Nature and Spiritual Development: Being in Nature and with Nature

No one can deny that feelings of wonder, awe, joy, and inner peace come to the forefront when children are in relationship with nature, whether they are spending time out in nature or nature is brought indoors for further exploration. Young children require time to explore natural environments. They need to see it, touch it, ask their own questions, and be given language to reinforce their own experiences. Nature simply makes children feel good and encourages them to truly use their senses (Gardner 1999). Simultaneously, nature touches human beings in a deep and spiritual way by providing us with wonder (Louv 2011). This chapter is all about the ways in which nature and spiritual development come together to stimulate our basic dispositions. Nature provides an excellent milieu for supporting a child's spiritual development.

Nature Education

The idea of nature education was born out of reports from nature educators from forest schools and garden schools that consistently provide children with a high quality of well-being (Armitage 2009; Änggård 2010). Swedish nature preschools use nature as a classroom space for learning through imaginative fairy play (Änggård 2010). Nature preschools also exist in the United States, where a school day might be spent outdoors exploring and playing in diverse habitats, such as meadows, streams, lakes, beaches, wooded areas, forests, and other available habitats. Some nature preschools also invite young children to participate in learning through extended projects or ongoing experiences, such as "maple sugaring, gardening, [caring for] nature center and/or farm animals, artifact collections, and special naturalist programs" (Bailie 2012, 136–37). Forest schools and garden schools both provide places for children to learn, play, and grow as children continue to develop an understanding of their relationship with the earth. No matter what type of school, all educators can and should introduce young children to nature in one way or another, especially if they hope to nurture children's spiritual development.

The Benefits of Nature for Young Children

Out of these nature-based educational settings comes research that documents the many benefits inherent in nature play. Being in nature appears to stimulate health by offering a variety and complexity of physical activity that helps children live healthier lives (Rivkin 2013). If children are playing outdoors, it means they are not sitting indoors watching TV or whining about something they want. It means they are active, moving, and engaged in a way that helps them to build on their own growing awareness of what they can and cannot do.

Spiritual Development in Action

BIG CLIMBING ROCK

Many years ago, I taught at a school that had a large rock in the playground. I was then working with four-year-olds. Some of the children were tall enough and strong enough to boost themselves onto the rock and then jump down. It was great fun until one of the other educators came up to me (I was a new educator at the school) and quietly told me that jumping from the rock was not allowed. I thanked her, as her gesture was intended to be helpful, but I had to question the reason for the rule. She simply responded, "Someone could get hurt." Again, I thanked her for the warning and said, "I don't think anyone will get hurt. Look at how well these children are jumping." I also shared with her my rule for creating a safe environment. I do not lift children—not for monkey bars, rocks, or other outdoor structures. I will lend a hand or demonstrate how to do something, but if children are not ready to get up on a structure by themselves, then in my mind they are not ready to be up there just yet. I was lucky that this individual appreciated my perspective, as I was being quite bold. But I have learned that this is an especially helpful rule when you are with an entire group of children. It is also lots of fun to encourage children to help one another and for children to notice their own and one another's growth in ability and in height and weight as time passes. The process of getting up on a rock is very complex and requires one's entire body. As an educator, I would not want to rob this amazing bodily experience from any child.

Spiritual Development in Action

HANGING FROM OUR TREE

At this same school, we had trees with low-lying branches.
At the beginning of each year, similar to the rock story, only
some of the children could reach the branches by themselves.
By the end of the year, all the children were tall enough to
swing themselves on the branches. The moment a child is tall
enough or big enough becomes a spiritual moment and a
reflection of personal growth and self-awareness.

Spending time in nature appears to foster emotional well-being and strengthens social bonds (Erickson and Ernst 2011; Rivkin 2013). Some believe that being in nature calms people and might help those with ADHD (Taylor, Kuo, and Sullivan 2002). Research also confirms that time spent in nature encourages higher creativity scores as reflected in the Torrance Tests of Creative Thinking (TTCT), which happens to be a better indicator for lifetime success than IQ tests or high school grades (Louv 2005). And still, there are other benefits. Nature brings people together. Love of nature connects children to ethical attitudes toward their environment, prevents children from feeling a fear of nature, and leads to *biophilia* or love of the earth (Moore and Marcus 2008; Bailie 2012). Biophilia helps guarantee that children will grow to be good stewards of the earth. Another term that describes our relationship with the earth is the *ecopsychological self*, which refers to a child's sense of self in relationship to the earth (Phenice and Griffore 2003). Kellert (2005) contended that both physical and mental well-being depended on the quality and quantity of one's experience with the natural world. This relationship is rooted in human biology that shapes a person's experiences, learning, and culture. Given that these processes begin early in life, Kellert turned his attention toward young children and nature as he studied children's emotional, intellectual, and evaluative development in relation to the environment.

Clearly, human beings need to have relationships with the earth. The question today is, what kind of relationship are educators and parents encouraging between young children and the earth? Are they friend or foe?

Spending time in nature has also been shown to boost brain development (Rivkin 2013). It appears that the human brain is "wired to pay attention to novelty, movement, intensity, contrast" (Jensen 2008, 55), qualities found in abundance in nature. For these reasons and more, children also need nature to stimulate their spiritual development. Furthermore, there is no reason all children cannot and should not have access and opportunity to experience nature at least some of the time during each day. This is especially true when nature is defined as "parks, views of trees and other vegetation, woods, fields, bits of green environments, yards, neighborhoods, and common outdoor spaces" (Rivkin 2013, 9). These can be found anywhere, even in the heart of a concrete city.

MINDFULNESS

Although the word *mindfulness* was not frequently used by educators in the grounded research study, it does conjure up a spiritual connection for many educators. As I speak about spiritual development to educators and school principals around the United States, they often respond by saying, "Oh yes, we offer mindfulness in our school program," as if to say they are indeed supporting a child's spiritual development. In a way, they are . . . at least they are taking one step closer in that direction. Interestingly, practicing mindfulness can also make a person feel as if he has just been out in nature. Practicing mindfulness and taking a walk in nature both are capable of putting breath, or spirit, back into one's body.

Dr. Ellen Langer (2014), sometimes referred to as the "mother of mindfulness" in the United States, defines mindfulness as an active state of mind when novelty or newness catches our attention.

Another goal of mindfulness is to achieve an acute awareness of the world and one's own place in it, similar to but slightly different from developing one's sense of self. Rather, being in nature invites children to find their own still, quiet, internal place. In fact, mindfulness leaders, such as Langer, believe that children who do not have opportunity to experience life in this way might be heading toward failure. Megan Cowan (2010), cofounder and codirector of the Oakland-based Mindful Schools program defines mindfulness as (1) awareness, in which each individual is capable of paying close attention to his own experiences using both the senses and the mind; (2) being nonjudgmental by not labeling things as good or bad but rather maintaining a neutral attitude; and (3) stillness of the heart and the mind. Mindfulness is also about reducing toxic stress—prolonged activation of stress to a child's biological system without the benefit of protective relationships. According to the Center on the Developing Child (accessed 2017), "toxic stress can have damaging effects on learning, behavior, and health across the lifespan." When practiced, mindfulness can lead children to emotional regularity, calmness, adaptability, and resilience. In other words, practicing mindfulness helps children to thrive while also preventing toxic stress.

But what if there is more we can do to prevent toxic stress, such as nurturing a child's spiritual development beginning at birth? Maybe mindfulness begins with an adult taking time to notice an infant's ability to focus on something meaningful, beautiful, or interesting to that child. When so engaged, infants have great capacity to focus. But these early skills are easily lost if they are not nurtured. We need to take time to observe these qualities in children, name them, and support them. Maybe for infants the question is, how can mindfulness be cultivated and grown from what is naturally present at birth? For babies who have a difficult time calming down, how can adults in these infants' lives use mindfulness and nature to help each child reach moments of calm?

Spiritual Development in Action

CALMING A BABY

One day I witnessed my three-month-old grandson crying. His father was holding him in the crook of his arm: head in hand, body lying parallel to his father's forearm. Baby and father were face-to-face. My son said to his child, "Ilan, you have just eaten, so I know you are not hungry. I have also changed your diaper, so I know you're not wet, and you just had a great nap. I really think you're okay." The baby looked himself over and then looked into his father's eyes—a deep I-Thou kind of look. In that instant, this child stopped crying.

Nance Rubel, a Cleveland therapist and expert on mindfulness, shares that a definition of mindfulness should include a statement about pausing and using your wisdom to think of a solution for yourself. Wisdom includes knowledge based on your own experience as well as intuition. Mindfulness can therefore be viewed as the growing wisdom of self that encourages people to adapt, just as my young grandson did when his father guided him through what might have been his first mindful experience.

Beyond these beginning stages of awareness, young children need caregivers to have high yet achievable expectations for them while simultaneously providing opportunities for children to experience great joy and wonder. Nature is a great playground for this to happen (Nell, Drew, and Bush 2013).

Nature combined with mindfulness also offers a way for children to connect their basic dispositions to their complex dispositions. Complex dispositions are made visible when children respond to external stimuli with acts of caring, kindness, empathy, and reverence. Again, each child will respond to different situations in different ways depending on her own unique internal complex disposition. What causes one person to respond with kindness can cause a very different reaction in another person. (Complex dispositions and prosocial words such as *caring*, *kindness*, *empathy*, and *reverence* will be explored more fully in chapter 6, "Preventing Bullying by Nurturing Spiritual Development.")

Susan Kaiser Greenland (2010), author of *The Mindful Child*, offers the ABCs of mindfulness: attention, balance, and compassion. Greenland's definition describes how young children might use their acute ability of awareness of senses to gather information from everything around them. Her definition comes closest to a system of spiritual development in which one's sense of self is developed alongside deep connections and strong relationships and in which a child's basic disposition is nurtured through moments of wonder, awe, joy, and inner peace. This leads to an awakening of a child's complex disposition reflected in her acts of caring, kindness, empathy, and reverence.

In the end, mindfulness is nothing new. The history of mindfulness stretches back to Buddhism, although its popularity for helping children is a relatively recent phenomenon and very popular today. Nurturing a child's spiritual development at the beginning of life may help children to learn to calm themselves while also supporting the development of their sense of self. This alone might help in preventing stress—or at least give children the tools to cope with stress.

Eventually, the practice of mindfulness can lead to calm, clarity, and compassion. The last word, compassion—defined as sympathy, empathy, concern, kindness, consideration, and care—parallels what Dr. Daniel Siegel (2010) terms *mindsight*.

MINDSIGHT

Mindsight offers another interesting and useful perspective as the relationship between mindfulness and spiritual development is explored. Looking at mindsight can also help us to better understand how and why nature is so important to human well-being and how mindfulness, mindsight, and nature all connect to nurture the spiritual development of young children.

Initially, *mindsight* meant experiencing feelings of empathy for other people and insight into oneself. This definition of mindsight included our ability to reflect, acknowledge, and understand ourselves as well as other people's feelings. Today, mindsight involves a third component: integration. Dr. Daniel Siegel, the person who coined the term *mindsight*, now defines it as insight, empathy, kindness, and compassion, along with a deep kind of integration. This integration consists of both internal and external harmony. He parallels this idea of harmony with the experience of either singing with or listening to a choir beautifully harmonizing the song "Amazing Grace." In such a harmony, each voice blends with the others but is still distinct (Siegel 2010).

Dr. Siegel believes that this type of integration is made possible when the brain, the regulator of the body, and the mind, the integrator, work together. By working together, the brain and the mind are capable of shaping our relationships, our learning, and our entire nervous system in a harmonious way.

What does this have to do with nature and spiritual development? Most people feel similar sensations of integration when they are outside in nature.

Connecting Nature and Spiritual Development

The spiritual aspect of mindfulness and mindsight is that humans are capable of having these very deep, significant feelings. These feelings touch our inner self, our essence, or our dispositions and help us to integrate our body, mind, and spirit. These same feelings are made possible when young children spend time in nature. Ultimately, the emotions felt might be described as wonderment, awe, joy, and inner peace (Louv 2005; Rivkin 2013). These feelings of connectedness and integration may lead us to act with caring, kindness, empathy, and reverence (Schein 2012). In this way, basic dispositions lead to the creation or emergence of complex dispositions.

DEFINING THE SPIRITUAL WORDS THAT NURTURE CHILDREN'S BASIC DISPOSITIONS

It is time to reflect on the language that describes our basic dispositions. What do all of these words—*wonderment, awe, joy,* and *inner peace*—actually mean? Is there a difference between wonder and wonderment, between wonderment and awe? What makes joy different? These are all important questions to ask if we use nature to evoke these feelings and then try to match the feeling and the experience with each child's disposition.

Wonder and Wonderment

As a noun, the word *wonder* refers to feelings of surprise mingled with respect or admiration stimulated by beauty, the unexpected, or the unfamiliar. As a verb, *wonder* implies a desire or curiosity to know something that leads to pondering and puzzlement of a big question. *Wonderment* reflects feelings of surprise or amazement, as when something out of the ordinary occurs. Such moments are plentiful in early childhood classrooms as all of life is new to young children.

Awe

Awe can also be used as a noun or a verb. It implies feelings of respect and wonder sometimes mixed with a little fear.

Joy

Joy is a word most often associated with feelings of pleasure and happiness. Happiness, according to Nel Noddings, should be a primary goal of education. Her research shows that happy people "learn better than unhappy ones... [and] are rarely mean, violent, or cruel" (Noddings 2007, 2). Happy people are better able to deal with the adversities that are a part of life. Noddings writes that "to be happy, human beings must have important needs satisfied" (4). Needs are differentiated from wants, as in our human need for relationships and friendship. Happiness can also be achieved by learning a skill, solving a problem, or exposing our complex dispositions of caring, kindness, empathy, and reverence to the world. One is apt to feel such emotions when one is either in nature or with nature.

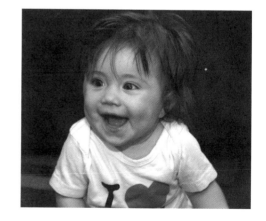

Spiritual Development in Action

MY FIRST NATURE RATTLE

Having studied about nature's impact on human beings, I was pondering how to bring nature into the inner-city programs I was consulting with. Sitting on my kitchen table were two distinct piles of intentional collections. One was recyclable plastic containers and the other pile contained pieces of nature I had collected while walking my dog. Just before walking out the door, I grabbed a plastic container, the kind that strawberries or blueberries come in at the grocery store. With the other hand, I reached for a few pinecones and acorns. I took some pretty duct tape I had lying around and created what I then called a nature rattle.

I have since offered many workshops on how to make nature rattles, now named *Nattles*. Here is a picture of a Nattle a teacher made. It is my way of helping educators and parents connect their children to nature.

I took the rattle into the school and, naturally, the children were drawn to it. My overall goal is not to hand the children something already made, but to encourage early childhood educators to go outdoors with their children to gather up natural materials to bring indoors. I know that even in the most urban neighborhoods one can always find glimpses of nature.

Spiritual Development in Action

STORY OF THE LADYBUGS

While working in inner-city Cleveland in the early 2000s, I was determined to find some nature for the children. We went on walks. We found three small parks within a few blocks of our school. One day, we discovered a place where ladybugs congregated. They were beautiful; most were red, but there were a few orange and yellow ones too. All but one or two children were daring enough to have the ladybugs land on their bodies, their arms, and their heads.

While walking back and forth to see the ladybugs, the children and I collected sticks and pebbles and leaves, whatever caught our fancy. We had a nature collection in our room that the children could explore, examine, or use in art projects, sorting, pattern making, and so on.

Once again, I witnessed children's faces aglow, similar to looks I had observed as my grandchildren wandered into imaginary play. I could only assume that something in this experience was touching the children in a very deep spiritual way.

SPIRITUAL SENSINGS

The relationship between nature and spiritual development runs deep. To highlight this, I turn to three types of "spiritual sensings" or realms where children experience interaction between the self and the external world: awareness-sensing, mystery-sensing, and value-sensing (Mata 2010).

Awareness-Sensing

Awareness-sensing occurs within self-awareness, or understanding one's own thought processes. Naturally, this type of conscious awareness does not seem to occur in very young children (or so we think), but nevertheless, brain research confirms that even though a child may not be consciously aware (or able to remember by recall) what they are experiencing or learning, their experiences greatly affect their development of self-awareness and metacognition. Therefore, one might say that awareness-sensing occurs as children build their understanding of what the world is by experiencing spiritual moments and amazing feelings of wonderment, awe, joy, and inner peace (Louv 2005; Rivkin 2013; Wilson 2014).

Mystery-Sensing

Mystery-sensing occurs when children have opportunities to use their imaginations while exploring and being in moments of wonder, wonderment, awe, joy, or inner peace. Mystery-sensing is especially helpful to children in overcoming fear of the unknown or the incomprehensible (Mata 2010). Mystery-sensing brings to mind moments of awe (wonder with a touch of fear).

Spiritual Development in Action

THE GRUFFALO

For one school in California, the children were convinced that the Gruffalo lived in the redwood tree forest next to their school. The Gruffalo is a fictitious character created by Julia Donaldson (1999) and Axel Scheffler. Evidently the children developed a passion for this book character and spent many hours outdoors searching the land for clues of its existence. If you were to speak to any of these children, they would quickly tell you that they indeed found the Gruffalo's bathroom, kitchen, and bedroom. They even left gifts for the Gruffalo. A true I-Thou relationship, albeit one-sided, grew out of the experience.

Other moments of awe might be more concrete.

Spiritual Development in Action

GOLDILOCKS AND THE THREE BEARS

I once taught at an urban school in a drug-infested neighborhood. I did my best to create a stimulating learning environment for the children. I used Montessori techniques to help children develop focusing skills. I was inspired by the Hundred Languages from Reggio Emilia educators. I provided small projects, documentation and drawing, lots of art and reflection, and lots of time outdoors too. We found spiderwebs, birds, ladybugs, and worms galore. When I introduced fairy tales, I sensed something was off. I soon came to realize that the concept of the forest was foreign to these children. I called the local arboretum and booked a field trip. When we arrived, the children were almost too frightened to go into the forest. By the end of the day, each child had gathered new information, new impressions, and had developed a new relationship with both the story of Goldilocks and the Three Bears and forests. Rather than fear, they were beginning to possess feelings of awe and wonderment and maybe even an appreciation for forests.

One participant in my research said, "I feel strongly about [children] having close contact with nature. They need to be immersed in piles of leaves and the sand on the beach. Their involvement in nature should also include their being active in the caring of these things and the caring of the natural world around them. This is one of the strongest ways to support spiritual development because there is that sense of beauty and mystery and that oneness in the natural world." This quote reflects the mystery of nature and the sense of awe and responsibility it is capable of instilling in young children, a belief shared with E. O. Wilson, creator of the word *biophilia*—love of the earth, love for life.

Value-Sensing

The third spiritual sensing, value-sensing, values feelings and emotions more than cognition. This is not to say that cognition is ignored. Rather, it implies, for me anyway, that cognition must build on a child's emotional and spiritual state. The children in my inner-city classroom were initially unable to understand the setting in the story of the three bears until they visited a forest. They were then able to learn about, appreciate, and differentiate a forest from other natural environments, such as a valley, hill, or lake. But first they had to rid themselves of fear of the unknown, which weighed heavily for some of them. Clearly, the beauty of forests and the connection they have to fairy tales would have been lost to these children if I had not valued the children's feelings over their cognitive development. This philosophy parallels Bronfenbrenner, Ainsworth, Maslow, and other theorists who believe that social and emotional development sometimes take precedence over cognitive development. Furthermore, wonder, awe, joy, and inner peace are triggered by experiences that touch a child's basic disposition just so. They are part of what can be considered spiritual moments.

All three sensings—awareness-sensing, mystery-sensing, and value-sensing—put a child's spiritual development in direct contact with the external world in which nature plays a predominant role. The natural milieu highlights a child's unique disposition and helps to make that disposition known to both child and educator. As always, each child's disposition will connect to nature in a unique way.

What Researchers Have to Say about Nature and Spiritual Development

Nature can inspire such feelings as childhood wonder. Wonder occurs when children view their natural world. Children have great internal ability to feel "presence, joy, and awareness" (Shafer 2004, 5). Moments of wonderment and joy are often experienced when children connect to plants, animals, and people beyond themselves. David Sobel (2016) offers a reminder that the spiritual benefits of nature do not have to be about God and religion but nonetheless offer children amazing views of the world. Ultimately, spirituality is evoked through internal feelings of wonder, wonderment, awe, joy, and inner peace or a desire to experience novelty, movement, intensity, or contrast, which often reflect the young child's inner disposition (Rivkin 2013).

REGGIO EMILIA'S PHILOSOPHY ON NATURE AND SPIRITUAL DEVELOPMENT

Reggio Emilia philosophy expands on Montessori's metaphor of the spiritual embryo and Buber's theory of I-Thou relationships by adding an understanding of children's need and desire to socially construct knowledge through language, big questions, and small-group investigations that often emerge directly from exploration in nature (Gandini et al. 2005; Lally, Mangione, and Greenwald 2006; Rinaldi 2006). Shadow, light, color, and water exploration are a few examples of investigatory play that delight and nurture children's spiritual development as they build personal and collective relationships with nature.

A recent quote on nature and Reggio Emilia philosophy appeared in the foreword of *Nature Education with Young Children: Integrating Inquiry and Practice*. The introduction was written by Dr. Lella Gandini, one of the leaders of the Reggio Emilia philosophy. She writes the following:

> I have asked myself: could a program for children—or a curriculum, as now seems to be the word of choice—be designed and constructed entirely on the basis of the experiences of children in these wondrous natural environments? Could we accompany children in their noticing of different shades of green? . . . Could we notice together the design,

harmony and balance in the structure of a tree, or of just a branch, or indeed of a leaf? (Gandini 2013, xiii)

In reading this quote, I am left feeling, as I often feel, that spirituality is quite compatible with Reggio Emilia philosophy. I am left wondering why so little is said about spiritual development. Just like in America, the Italians seem to have no language for discussing spirituality, or perhaps not that much interest. So I took it upon myself to act as "teacher researcher."

HOWARD GARDNER AND SPIRITUAL INTELLIGENCE

Howard Gardner is best known for his popular theory of multiple intelligences. His first seven intelligences include linguistic, logical-mathematical, musical, spatial, bodily kinesthetic, interpersonal, and intrapersonal (Gardner 1993). He did not mention nature or spirituality or existential intelligences. Eventually, after years of creating and testing to a specific criterion, Gardner decided to include spiritual intelligence within naturalistic intelligence. Spiritual intelligence is also connected to existential intelligence, which is defined as a partial intelligence (Gardner 1999). In Gardner's view, existential intelligence is the human tendency to ponder the fundamental question all cultures ask about existence (Gardner 2006). In fact, many people define spiritual development as interconnected with existence or as a philosophical exploration of existential intelligence. By the time a child is old enough to ask questions about existence, Gardner believes that he is already fairly indoctrinated into his culture and has adopted a philosophical stance (Gardner 1993). Nevertheless, both naturalistic and existential intelligences imply that moments spent in wonder, awe, joy, and inner peace, or asking big questions that can take children beyond themselves, can go a long way toward nurturing a child's spiritual development.

LEV VYGOTSKY AND THE NEED FOR LANGUAGE TO SPEAK ABOUT NATURE AND SPIRITUAL DEVELOPMENT

Educators are beginning to see the nurturing of a child's spiritual development as a way to support the development of a child's sense of self, which leads children to explore their surroundings. Knowledgeable, supportive, and responsive educators can create an optimal environment for exploration. Adding language to experiences invites children to give meaning to their intrapersonal and interpersonal experiences (Gardner 1999) and to the awe, wonderment, joy, and sense of self they are developing. Thought and language help children appreciate and connect with all that is beyond themselves. Children internalize their understandings (Vygotsky 1962). From this type of awareness, children build on a sense of self, developing a will, motivation, ethical understanding, and a sense of responsibility (Montessori 1967; Kagan 2004). This is why it is so important to look at words and experiences together and to attempt to figure out what it all means.

Conclusion: Reflections about Nature and Spiritual Development

Daniel Meier and Stephanie Sisk-Hilton (2013, 2) go on to say that "what really matters in nature education [is] calling on children's powers of attention and focus, of wonderment and joy, analysis and reflection, individual exploration and collaborative discovery, and sifting and sorting of information, data, and concepts over time." Rachel Carson, marine biologist, conservationist, and author, wrote of her hope for every child to have at least one adult to discover and share the world with in the book *Silent Spring*. To this, Tobin Hart (2006, 168) adds his belief that sharing joys, excitement, and mysteries with children can actually "shape a worldview and even change the course of one's life."

This is how important it is for educators and parents to think about the relationship between nature and spiritual development. We can shape the world for future generations so that they too can live in a world filled with wonder. When we address spiritual development, we look at the deepest reasons for why humans need nature. Being in nature also provides us with an ability to become peaceful cohabitants of the earth. To provide these moments for young children, we must pay closer attention to the kind of environments we are providing.

Furthermore, the Earth Charter Initiative (accessed 2017) calls for peace and defines peace as "the wholeness created by right relationships with oneself, other persons, other cultures, other life, Earth and the larger whole of which we are a part." The conception of an Earth Charter began after a meeting of the World Commission on Environment and Development in 1987 in the hopes of creating guidelines for sustainable development. For me, this is even more reason for early childhood educators to support children's spiritual bond with nature and the earth. So where do we begin? My research suggests that a good starting point is to create spiritual moments and rich environments.

THINGS TO DO TO NURTURE CHILDREN'S RELATIONSHIP WITH NATURE

☀ Ask children to share how it feels to take a deep breath or to breathe slowly. Encourage deep breathing at some point each day for yourself and children. Here are some other breathing ideas to practice with children:

— Have children breathe on a mirror or exhale warm air outdoors on a cold day.

— Help children to follow their breath as it moves throughout the body to the head, toes, and fingers.

— Breathe slowly together with one or two children. Encourage them to watch how their bodies move in and out with each breath.

— Invite children to explore their bodies for places from which air escapes (nose, mouth).

— Notice how the simple act of taking a deep breath can change how you feel.

☀ Provide a classroom environment that encourages focus on natural elements.

— Provide bowls of seashells or assortments of leaves, rocks, sticks, and the like. Watch to see what catches each child's attention.

— Change it up by adding new attractions during the year.

— If a child loves rocks, go to the library and check out *A Collaboration with Nature* by Andy Goldsworthy. Start a classroom collection of rocks.

☼ Give time for children to be alone and present, to play without being told what to do, to have time to be with materials and/or friends that they love.

☼ Ask children to describe what they see, hear, smell, and touch during a walk on the beach, in the woods, and so on.

☼ Spend some alone time in the morning before interacting with the children to allow yourself time to be present.

☼ Go outside every day!

CHAPTER 5

Cultivating Spiritual Moments with Young Children

WHEN I INITIALLY ASKED early childhood educators to describe the kinds of spiritual activities and experiences they provide for young students, most of them were speechless. They said that they had no words to describe spiritual activities or they had no idea what was being asked of them. At first, I believed that this was an indication that spiritual development simply was not occurring in early childhood classrooms across the United States. I have since come to understand that the question was not well worded. It did not tap the educators' perceptions of what they actually do every day with and for children. What good early childhood educators consistently do is create "spiritual moments." But without a language for talking about spiritual development, an awareness of these moments and the environment needed to create them often goes unnoticed. Many educators today still have no idea that they may actually be nurturing children's spiritual development.

The question becomes clearer when I ask, "Have you ever seen a child's face light up with pure inner excitement and wonder?" We have all been privileged to witness such moments. Children's faces can shine in response to many types of moments. This happens when something external touches the child internally in a way that connects with her disposition, providing her with feelings of wonderment, awe, joy, or inner peace. These are the kinds of moments that will be discussed in this chapter.

Transforming a Classroom into a Spiritual Space

Below is a picture of a school in which I once taught. When I walked into the room, I could see the potential hidden within the clutter. Every classroom has this potential. I have shared these photos at workshops to guide and encourage educators to clean up their classrooms, to make their space inviting both for the children's sake and for theirs. This is *not* the milieu Schwab was going for. But watch the transformation.

In the photo at the top of page 93, there is still some work to be done. My colleague and I moved the table so it was parallel to the wall. The minute we made this change, a child walked in and began discussing the meaning of the Van Gogh poster hanging in the background. I have learned that placement is everything if you want children to connect and explore different aspects of the classroom. Eventually, the alphabet posters above on the wall were removed, and all the walls, once painted in bright primary colors, were painted white. Finally, a platform was built by a father of children in the school. It truly takes a village to create a beautiful classroom.

Many early childhood educators now know how important the environment is for scaffolding learning in early childhood education. In the fall of 2016, I showed these photographs at a workshop I was presenting at an early childhood conference. One of the participants raised her hand and said, "I hate to tell you this, but the first classroom picture you showed us is what my classroom looks like, and so do most other classrooms I visit." I know she is right because I do consulting across the country and this is often what I see. I am not showing the photo here as an insult or to tell educators that what they are doing is wrong; rather, I am sharing this image in the hopes that early childhood educators will begin to understand and to use this model as an inspiration for creating more beautiful spaces for their children and themselves. Educators should never forget that they too are part of the equation. Once I learned this, I began to bring things into my own classrooms that I truly loved. Some of my favorite additions were turtles, potato plants, a picture of Van Gogh's *Sunflowers*, peacock feathers, and a large bird feeder outside the window. Making environmental changes is hard but not as difficult as it is to live in a messy room without anything that makes you smile.

Spiritual Development in Action

TODDLER CLASS WITH MESSY BOOKS

For two years straight, I worked with an early childhood educator in a room for two-year-olds. She asked to work with me because she was seeking help in time management and room organization. After spending some time going in circles, she and I hit on something small and concrete she might do to implement change. She took out the bookshelf that was less than functional because it was impossible for the children to put books back on the shelf without the books falling onto the floor. The bookshelf was replaced with a shorter, wider shelf that held the books the children brought to it. The children and their educator also took time to sort large books from small books. The ultimate goal was for the children to help keep the room clean by putting books back properly—fronts showing, right-side up.

This is actually where the word *reverence* applies in relation to spiritual development in a classroom setting. It is all about respect, purpose, and a sense of order. When a child is able to show enough respect to place a book back onto the bookshelf properly, how much more able is that same child to show respect to a friend, an educator, a parent? How much closer is this child to showing reverence for the earth and for the world?

To this day, this educator runs to give me a big hug whenever I see her. She says to me, "You are the one who taught me about respect and how to show my two-year-olds how to achieve it." It is a sweet memory in my own memory bank.

It is also quite helpful and wonderful if your classroom environment has a designated area to call an art studio. A similar type of order is needed as in the picture on page 94, but it is also a place of busyness, messiness, and creativity. The order of the sorted containers invites children to achieve great creative powers. An art studio should hold within its walls the Hundred Languages available for children's exploration. From this place, great projects might unfold where children work together in small groups to seek answers to their very big questions. When one explores the world of art, whether it is graphic art, dance, music, and so on, spiritual development is being nurtured.

I have one more thought to share about environments, or milieu. In Reggio Emilia approaches, you might have heard reference to the phrase "environment is the third teacher." The concept of the environment as a third teacher is very powerful and helpful. When your environment works as an educator, you will suddenly discover that you have fewer behavior problems, if any. This is because beautiful, well-organized classrooms invite children to remain busy, intentional, focused, and engaged. Such classrooms abound with spiritual moments.

Defining Spiritual Moments

The idea of spiritual moments is captured by these educators' words. One educator said, "When you see [a spiritual moment], you know it. But if we are not paying attention, we can even miss it, not even recognize it. Emotions, feeling from the core, reflection, pondering, deep peace, [and] inner contentment all seem to be a part of a spiritual moment." Another educator said, "I have those moments every day. I have taught for over twenty years. Those moments happen very fast: the eye contact, the physical contact."

Still another educator shared what might be on many people's minds. She said that culturally, the language often used in connection to spirituality is the language of religion. After a long pause, she continued: maybe part of our problem is the lack of language.

During my research study on spiritual development in early childhood education, I identified five different types of spiritual moments: spiritual moments in time, in space, in and with nature, in strong relationships, and with big questions capable of taking each individual beyond oneself. It is important for educators and parents to understand that these distinctions are needed so that we, the adults in a child's life, can be attuned to the spiritual needs of each child. The children themselves experience these moments in complete integration as they play and learn (Lally, Mangione, and Greenwald 2006).

SPIRITUAL MOMENTS IN TIME

Spiritual moments in time refer to children's need to spend some part of each day in quiet, calm moments, where they have extended time to play and explore their world. Spiritual moments in time also implies a set routine and order to both the classroom and the schedule so that children do not have to take time to second-guess what it is they are expected to do or know. They simply are in this moment, and it belongs to them.

I have a favorite photograph depicting my vision of a spiritual moment in time. In that picture, two small boys are leisurely looking out a large window that oversees a grassy piece of yard in front of a street on which cars are passing by. The window is open, and there appears to be a lovely quality

of air flowing through. The boys seem to be enjoying simply being in the moment. A small girl is standing next to a low platform built for block construction. She is using soft foam blocks and has already created a rather tall and sturdy structure. She is holding two blocks in her hand as she seems to contemplate where to place them. The room has plants, pictures, and designated spaces for specific activities to take place. Yet the children have complete freedom of choice and movement within the space. To me, there is no rush, no hurry to get anything done. There is time to breathe, to feel present in the moment. The clothes the children are wearing give signs of the seasonal time. It must be spring or early fall because the boys are wearing short-sleeved shirts and the girl has on a light dress and no tights. It is like a Norman Rockwell painting of the '90s.

Another photo I have shows a small child who had been spending lots of time each day opening and closing a small saltshaker. In the photo, something in this process has captured his attention, is massaging his fine muscles, and is guiding him to focus so that his whole being is involved in the task. If you close your eyes, you can picture that look of intense concentration. To an untrained eye or to someone simply passing by, it might look like nothing important is happening. But for an educator who is looking for spiritual moments in time, this is it. This child is in a zone of complete integration. The saltshaker has become a Thou for the child and will continue to be until he masters whatever it is he is intent on knowing. Such moments should not be interrupted.

When playing within spiritual moments in time, children can discover and experience a kind of flow where the need to stay on schedule or accomplish certain tasks is suspended. Young children can meander and explore inner thoughts and dive into self-chosen experiences. This special time can include listening, being still, or being very active. A child's disposition comes into play, making this an exceptionally fruitful time for educators and parents to learn about a child's inner thoughts, images of self, and developmental progress through unobstructed, knowledgeable observation. *This means that the observing adult must know about development and how to collect, record, and use helpful and important observations of children.*

Many techniques and tools can be used for collecting such observations. During my years in the classroom, I kept a clipboard close by to record my observations of children. (Today, educators might choose an iPad or a phone.) I would record comments, what I saw taking place, how children interacted with one another, choices children made in the given environment, and so on, for each child on a daily basis. This provided me with a running record of what was taking place. It also helped me to uncover each child's innate disposition and other valuable information about each child. These observations also provided me ideas for the next day, week, or month. Most importantly, observations help adults to uncover the valuable and important questions children might be pondering. These questions are often made visible when children have time—spiritual moments in time.

The idea of spiritual moments in time evolved directly from interviews I did with early childhood educators. One educator said children require "slow time during the day. Some educators, parents, and caregivers neglect to offer children open-ended time to play—or just be—because of a fear of boredom."

Another educator shared a new appreciation or interpretation for the word *boredom*, a word commonly used by American children. She told me that her reply to children who complained they were bored was, "Oh, how wonderful—you have time to ponder!"

Another educator mentioned the importance of giving children "time to be listened to, time to do whatever it is they have been doing, time to engage in beautiful art." This example showed a spiritual moment embedded in an art activity.

Following are some comments made by educators as they described their views on the importance of calm, order, and beauty in early childhood settings or environments. Beauty in these cases refers to children working and playing in environments that are physically organized and pleasing.

One said, "I come from a Montessori background, so I believe in order— that the environment needs to be beautiful, orderly, and comfortable. Everything has a place, and there is a place for everything." Another stated, "I was thinking about beauty in a classroom. The result is a calming, pleasing, and settled atmosphere."

Yet another asserted:

> We try to provide a calm, organized, safe, joyful experience for our boys and girls. We should challenge them with a [stimulating] environment but in a very calm way. We want them to know that they are safe in the environment. We want them to be stimulated and challenged. We want them to read books that have a message. We want to treat children with kindness and respect. And we want children to know that we appreciate them. We celebrate them. And we respect them. And I think in doing that, hopefully we are nurturing the positive things parents started at home.

The previous participant described well-known benchmarks for any early childhood program: activities that are organized, safe, and joyful. The difference is that she connected these actions and beliefs with the child's spiritual development. Unfortunately, this connection isn't the norm. Instead, what often occurs, according to one study participant, is the following:

> We are so caught up with standards and Step Up that sometimes we don't have the time to actualize the goodness within ourselves. There is no checklist for this; it gets lost in the craziness of what we do. It is

there, but I think sometimes it just gets lost among the other things that I think are much less important. To be honest, it's the pressure that gets in the way.

Another educator said, "No adult could work in an environment where there is no break from the noise, busyness and deadlines, and the quota-driven expectations. Children need breaks as well."

This is why it is important to begin thinking about spiritual moments in time. When early childhood educators and parents offer their children such moments, they are supporting the children's spiritual development.

Finally, spiritual moments in time reflect mindfulness. It is understandable that many educators who have not studied or thought much about spiritual development see mindfulness as the same as spiritual development. This is where mindfulness is found: in spiritual moments in time.

SPIRITUAL MOMENTS IN SPACE

Spiritual moments in space emerge out of spiritual moments in time because they require educators and parents to think about the environment in which the child is spending time. Spiritual moments in space occur in educational settings where objects, furniture, light, color, and space all come together to create a milieu that is considered beautiful, inviting, and appealing for the exploration and learning of young children. It is an environment purposefully designed to call to the children in a spiritual way. It invites the children to explore and interact so that their experiences might provide spiritual nurturing to their inner dispositions. Such spaces are often created by placing objects in the environment in a way that both displays the objects and invites the children to engage with them. Remember the goose? Terms such as the *Hundred Languages, aesthetics, beauty, intentionality,* and *perspective* are often used to describe spiritual moments in space.

Rocks and Spirituality

One year, I found myself working in a beautiful classroom. I brought in a basket of rocks thinking that the children would love them. I placed the basket of rocks on a shelf but no one touched them. I remember someone saying to me, "If the children are not interested, change things up." So one morning I decided to place the basket of rocks in the middle of the large window right above the longest blocks. I turned my back for no more than five minutes, and when I looked again, the rocks had been sorted into two piles.

For me, this is a small example of spiritual moments in space. Remember chapter 1 on love and a sense of self? Most of what children do relates back to this theme as well. Thus, changing the placement of the rocks invited at least one child to begin a relationship with these rocks.

Here is what educators had to say that led to the idea of spiritual moments in space:

My classroom is a well-designed space equipped with a wide variety of art materials—paint, pens, paper, clay, wire, beads, shells, and other natural materials. Children use these materials to create short- and long-term projects, giving them the opportunity to express themselves.

Typically, we American early childhood educators have tried to fill the environment with scientific explanations when, quite frankly, I think we should be creating environments that could be producing questions, wonderment, and curiosity about the world rather than answers to things. To teach children their colors appeals to the lowest part of brain development, not to mention a real lack of spiritual development or cognitive development. You reduce it to a name of a particular kind of color that robs all of the other possibilities.

I am constantly searching for a way to utilize materials not only for the purpose for which they were intended but also for new and exciting ways that they can be implemented or observed. I believe I take this philosophy into the classroom and that one of the joys of teaching is that students are never jaded in their approach to materials. They offer us a window into that world where everything is new and possibilities are endless. Isn't this why a large cardboard box has so much more resonance for children than electronic toys often do? It can unlock the imagination and expand horizons.

The use of the word *joy* makes this a particularly poignant example of a spiritual moment in space. Each child should find some element of joy in his classroom based on his own unique disposition. This simply means that for a child who loves rocks, rocks should be in the classroom. It does not mean that you inundate your classroom with commercial materials and plastic junk toys because this is what children are asking for. Rather, it means that you create your classroom environment carefully so that it can be sure to provide great and meaningful moments of wonderment, awe, joy, and inner peace.

Dressing Up and Spirituality

One year after winter break I decided to rid my classroom of Disney princess dresses. I wouldn't have minded them so much if the children were using them to dramatize stories. Instead, they were a source of competition and stress—who got to wear which dress. Then a hierarchy developed in which the alpha girl always wore the most coveted dress. The children at the lower end of this structure were left to find scraps to wear. We tried using the situation as a provocation for discussing fairness, kindness, sharing, and so on. Nothing worked, so I decided to take the dresses out of the room. Yes, I was nervous. I wondered what the girls would do all day.

The first day back after the long break, the girls entered the classroom and instantly noticed that the dresses were gone. I had replaced the commercial costumes with beautiful scarves and pieces of animal-print fabric and fake fur. We had been reading fairy tales before the break, so I placed a *Goldilocks and the Three Bears* book near the dress-up clothes. By the end of the week, the entire class was involved in creating a production of *Goldilocks and the Three Bears*. The project was a great success and a testimony for me as to how a beautiful space can inspire great projects and solid learning.

Spiritual moments in space are most often intentional. One educator said, "There is intentionality involved. I want the students to smell beautiful fragrances from real flowers, to marvel at the variety of vegetation around our building, to hear the songs of different birds when we go outside, and so on. Will they necessarily select the same objects of beauty as I do? Possibly not, and that is the joy of teaching."

Almost every educator I spoke to during my research study mentioned the value of nature and outdoor space as a source for spiritual moments.

Nature offers beauty, provides provocation for new questions, and can provide many moments of wonderment, awe, joy, and inner peace that can nurture each person's disposition in ways that help to nurture a child's spiritual development.

A Waldorf educator and participant in the study shared that Waldorf rooms are absolutely beautiful; the colors, the materials are all human-made from all-natural materials. Everything is given lots of care and thought. She also described a nature table that held real pressed flowers and seeds for next year's growing season. "Even food," she said. "We serve the food on china

plates." Everything is done with such care and reverence for the children and for the environment. The environment is created by the teacher who also takes time to work on her own spiritualness. Another educator said, "Spaces need to display a sanctuary for quiet moments so you can actually reflect. Set up your classroom in ways that invite children to engage with materials in ways that do not reflect the hustle and bustle" of the adult world. Children can also be taught to be reflective, mindful, and contemplative. These skills can be a gift to children in that they too help to nurture one's own inner disposition. The environment should provide for such a space.

Like many early childhood educators, I would often provide a space for such quiet meditation. One year I brought in a small tent, and my colleague's classroom of children built a cave out of boxes. Both spaces added a dimension of nature to the indoor space and sectioned off parts of the room for children to be alone and/or to play creatively within small groups. The more children can know about themselves, the more inner control they can achieve, the better friend they can be to others.

SPIRITUAL MOMENTS IN RELATIONSHIP TO OTHERS

Often, a child's relationship with nature will provide the inner joy and feelings of happiness that can open her up to deep and lasting human relationships. The same is true of spiritual moments in time and space. All provide moments for children to be in relationship with others and with themselves. While in relationships, children have many opportunities to receive kindness and to reciprocate acts of kindness. They practice ways to show respect, use empathy, experience harmony, and practice using a happy demeanor. They also develop listening skills and practice being welcoming to others. In other words, spiritual moments in relationship with others are where one practices being a caring, kind, and empathetic person.

One educator defined spiritual moments in relationships as "empathy, displays of kindness, and feelings of harmony." A second said, "When I see a child doing something counter to what would be self-serving—handing a toy they wanted to use to someone else to use first—that is a spiritual moment." A third said, "When I see a child spontaneously comfort another, or attempt to bring a child on the fringe of an activity into the group, those are spiritual moments." A fourth said, "I would say that a beautiful early childhood classroom is one that communicates clearly its values and expectations and reflects a respectful, positive, and powerful image of the child, family, and teacher. It promotes and nurtures relationships. It provides for

connectivity among all the protagonists and within the community and the natural world." For her, "attentiveness to the interrelatedness of all living beings" was an element that connected children's relationships to spiritual development.

Another educator added to these sentiments when she spoke about harmony as a reflection of a "spiritually beautiful" environment, which for her would be one where children and staff interact in harmonious ways, are kind and respectful to one another, and feel safe and at home.

In other words, the classroom is viewed as a sacred space for spiritual moments to occur, where relationships between teacher and student are deemed sacred. Of course, these spiritual moments go beyond this one relationship.

An educator said, "We create sacred space when we sit on the sofa with our arm around the child to read a book and listen to her comments." Maybe this is why reading to children has such a strong impact on their success as learners. Maybe it is also supporting the child's spiritual development.

Another educator said, "We take the time every school day to engage in personal conversation with each student, ask them to tell us what they were thinking when they drew a picture, or when we put a bandage on a scratch that we can barely see. If we respond to every student in that way, I believe we are beginning to create sacred space." This means the classroom and school should also be welcoming.

An educator shared that she thinks the environment plays a very important role in spiritual development because it speaks to children about being valued, welcomed, and respected. The environment can tell a child that he is a competent, creative person. I have to say that many schools I have visited present themselves as depicting a friendly milieu. But if there is not a director or an educator greeting each family as they come into the building each morning, then the school may not be as friendly as they think. If teachers are talking about one another or about other children in the hallways, or worse, in the classrooms, then that school is not a friendly, welcoming space. Remember the term *absorbent mind*? Nothing goes unnoticed by the children. The only way to be consistently friendly is to actually be authentically friendly. Having beautiful objects in the classroom can help maintain the good vibes of a friendly school. The children will see this too.

What sometimes worked for me was to privately think of the most positive quality of each person I was with. This way I could stay true to myself and remain in a positive relationship with whomever I was with. I must be honest: this is an area where I feel vulnerable. I share that because, ultimately, each educator must truly know her own strengths and vulnerabilities. Each of us must hone our ability to be reflective educators, not just for the children and their families but also for ourselves.

SPIRITUAL MOMENTS IN RELATION TO BIG QUESTIONS

Spiritual moments in relation to big questions refers to the kinds of questions that can help children see beyond themselves. Such big questions are capable of making young people feel transcendent and deeply connected to the world. The word *transcendence* comes from the Latin word meaning *climbing over* and is used today to reflect that which goes beyond or above the range of what might be considered a normal physical human experience.

For individuals who would like to put God and religion into a discussion of spiritual development, this is a good entry point; although transcendence can also be experienced without being in relationship to God or religion. This is beyond the scope of my study. For nonreligious transcendence, one simply feels something beyond oneself, whatever that may be—nature, a web of connectedness, feeling integrated with others, and so on. Some scholars believe that young children cannot truly realize the meaning of transcendence, but, in her work, Jennifer Mata describes facial expressions on kindergarten students that would beg to disagree. In the end, the idea of transcendence helps religious families connect to spiritual development. For those who do not seek a religious connection to spiritual development, transcendence can also be found in big questions. It is often through inquiry of such questions that children see the connection or web that connects one idea or system to another. It is often through big ideas that a child finds more questions, more wonder, and a stronger sense of his own smallness in the vastness of the world.

A big question full of ideas can show a child radical amazement (Heschel 1955). In his books, Abraham Joshua Heschel speaks of amazing moments of wonder and radical amazement that parallels E. O. Wilson's ideas about

biophilia (people's love for and connection to the earth). Together, Abraham Joshua Heschel and E. O. Wilson speak as theologian and scientist, respectively, of the great mysteries and wonders of the universe of which we are part.

Therefore, spiritual moments in relationship to big questions lead and encourage children to ask a myriad of questions. They provide place, space, and time for them to explore the world in their own way. Experiencing spiritual moments through big questions can help children feel as if they are indeed part of the world and not separate from it.

Such big questions were shared by some of the educators interviewed for the grounded theory study. One educator said, "I think that children, when they are outside, even though they are young, that there is something beyond themselves that can be bigger than themselves. Sort of a sense of wonder. How did it all get put there? And a lot of questions that come up like—why does the world look and function the way that it does?"

Another educator said, "Separate and apart from cognitive development, [spiritual development] helps children to keep exploring. You know when their whole sense of inquiry is pulled into this as they ask something and then keep going further and further. They don't give up, because even without answers there is something that moves them on. I think it is their spirituality that moves them on. It's the cognitive that sparks curiosity, spurring spiritual experiences."

Conclusion: Spiritual Moments—Where Spiritual Development Happens

The concept of spiritual moments might have been one of the most valuable findings of the grounded research study. I, for one, discovered that spiritual development does not rely on activities and experiences, as one might think about classroom-based learning, but on so much more. It is about offering children significant time, beautiful spaces, authentic relationships, quality time in and with nature, and the opportunity to think, articulate, and explore big questions. Together, spiritual moments provide a foundation by which a young child's spiritual development can continue. In other words, the child's spiritual embryo that exists at birth can continue to thrive when given the gift of spiritual moments.

THINGS TO DO TO NURTURE SPIRITUAL MOMENTS AMONG CHILDREN

- ☼ Create classroom environments that invite spiritual moments to occur. To do so, the environments must be built on the dispositions of the children in your classroom. This requires you to deeply know each child.

- ☼ Structure your day so there is time to breathe deeply and to be present and mindful.

- ☼ Create a sense of order so children know where to find what they need when they need it so they might create a spiritual moment for themselves.

- ☼ Invite and expect children to help keep the environment clean and tidy. Otherwise it is difficult either to find a spiritual moment or to create one.

☼ Be sure to have nature in your room—plants, animals, rocks, shells, sticks, acorns, and the like. Avoid plastic toys and commercial products.

☼ Use recyclables or loose parts for creativity, to save the earth, and to offer unusual relationships and moments for children.

☼ Know what brings feelings of wonder, awe, joy, and inner peace to the children in your classroom, and invite these feelings to happen in some way every day for them and for yourself.

☼ Keep your senses open to children's big questions and help them do the same.

☼ Come to the classroom ready to provide spiritual moments for children by having spent some time in a spiritual space yourself before coming to school.

CHAPTER 6

Preventing Bullying by Nurturing Spiritual Development

Nurturing children's spiritual development beginning at birth can have positive effects on a child's overall well-being and behavior. The development of will, resiliency, collaboration, mindfulness, values, and morals is all connected to this system of spiritual development through a child's complex dispositions. When children reach this stage of spiritual development, it is safe to say that they will also have developed a strong foundation of self-awareness and strong relationships, as well as respect for their relationships. They will have spent lots of time within spiritual moments, helping them develop a tendency to do what is expected, and hopefully, even a desire to do so at least some of the time. In other words, when children reach a stage of development where awareness of complex dispositions come into play, their ability to act kindly and empathetically is already present. These are not qualities found in children who bully. Children who bully, according to Emily Bazelon's (2013) book *Sticks and Stones*, are those who repeat physical or verbal acts of aggression toward others. They also use harassment and often do not display empathy. I believe that the roots of bullying behavior start early in life. I am also proposing that children may actually begin bullying because they have not been nurtured spiritually.

Robert Coles and many other theorists have often written about the importance of spiritual development. Amitai Etzioni, James Fowler, Howard Gardner, Maria Montessori, and Peter Senge wrote about the power of human spirituality, its presence at birth, and the positive role it can play in developing a whole, well-balanced child. Using terms such as *empathy*, *caring*, *kindness*, and *wonderment*, Etzioni as well as Gardner, Mihaly Csikszentmihalyi, and William Damon indirectly imply that nurturing a child's spirituality can lead to the creation of a "good society." Participants in my research study also found a connection between behavior and spiritual development. What if it were possible to nurture children so that caring, kindness, empathy, and reverence could naturally emerge as children grow and learn to be spiritual human beings?

Gardner and Multiple Intelligences

These new ideas about spiritual development would not be possible without the questions posed by Harvard psychologist Howard Gardner. In the early 1960s, psychology at Harvard was moving away from behaviorism toward cognitive psychology. At the time, Gardner made two observations. First, he shared that he was perplexed about the lack of focus on brain research, and he also realized that most developmentalists seemed to think that scientific thought and careers in science "represented the pinnacles or 'end-states' of human cognitive development" (Gardner 1999, 28). In other words, Gardner believed psychologists of his time were saying that there was only one way to be smart, and that meant becoming a scientist. Gardner broke this code by redefining intelligence as having multiple outlets. He moved away from intelligence being "what the tests test" (13) in favor of the ability to "solve problems or create products that are of value in a culture" (34). In other words, Gardner's redefined intelligences were seen as having potential for processing information that could be activated in a cultural setting to solve problems or create products of value for the overall culture. This view places Gardner in the same school of thought as Vygotsky, who viewed development as sociohistorical. Gardner and Vygotsky's work is reflected today in thoughts about open-ended materials, the project approach to learning, and the value of language to help guide a child's learning.

Gardner's theory of multiple intelligences has continued to evolve. Beyond grappling with a place to put spiritual intelligence, Gardner began to think of ways to merge his new understandings of intelligences and brain research with human decisions that are both moral and good. Some of his latest research focuses on adults doing "good work" (Gardner, Csikszentmihalyi, and Damon 2001).

Gardner believes that each individual has a unique intelligence profile. His work suggests that each individual possesses different basic and complex dispositions that connect their inner self internally and externally to their world. These qualities are described within interpersonal intelligence (between self and others) and intrapersonal intelligence (knowing oneself). And yet there is more.

Gardner suggests that learning should be individualized because everyone learns differently, and teaching should be pluralized, meaning that important concepts must be taught several different ways. Pluralism can also reflect ideas around social constructivism—the theory humans learn better in social settings. Gardner's beliefs about pluralism connect to his ideas for a more peaceful society in that life on earth should not and cannot be just about me but rather about us.

Taking Another Look at Children's Complex Dispositions

Building from Gardner's work, the ultimate goal of nurturing spiritual development in young children can be realized—thus creating good people, whole people, and well-functioning people. To do this, we must return to a discussion of children's complex dispositions. Complex dispositions are not necessarily taught. They can be entirely dispositional, such as in the naturally kind child. They can be modeled, as in families who are nice to others and therefore raise children who are nice. Or complex dispositions can be willed or chosen either unconsciously or consciously by the child.

From close observations of children, Montessori was able to describe her views of how a child's complex dispositions will develop. As a child's actions become deliberate and known to the child, the force referred to earlier as the spiritual embryo grows stronger. The child begins to "act consciously and voluntarily" (Montessori 1967, 253). Sometimes Montessori refers to a child's "unconscious knowing." A child's growing ability to focus and act intentionally also clearly affects a child's relationships, interactions, and the ability to learn and to act kindly toward others.

AN OBSERVATION OF CHILDREN TODAY

Over the years, I have noticed that children in the United States are coming to early childhood programs less able to focus and to find something that interests them. I have even heard from educators at conferences and workshops that children are coming into their classrooms not knowing how to play, not showing care for others or objects. I think this problem goes back to what Howard Gardner was saying: there are many different ways to explore the world, and we should not remain focused only on the academic/cognitive side of learning and knowing. We should not think of children as needing to develop executive functioning as if they were part of the business world. Instead, we should be talking about and thinking about children's many competencies and strengths. From my perspective, we should also be talking about children's spiritual development. Here are some photos of what very young children are capable of doing.

After giving a hands-on workshop about spirituality and nature to a small group of early childhood educators, I invited one of the educators to take the basket of rocks we had just used into her classroom of two-year-olds. She looked at me as if I were crazy. Then she said, "But they will throw the rocks." My answer to her was twofold. First, I suggested she give some real thought to where she might place the basket of rocks. Second, I suggested that she demonstrate how the rocks should be loved and respected.

She took me up on the first suggestion. She got to school early the next day and tried out several places. The place that worked best from her perspective was the platform table usually occupied by the trains. The educator shared a concern with me. One little boy would make a beeline to the trains

each morning. She was wondering what he would do when he found his trains had been moved. I convinced her to give it a try.

After greeting the children, we both observed as they entered the classroom. The little boy who played with the trains simply pulled the trains out and found a nice cozy place on the hard floor. One little boy, the one the educator was afraid would throw the rocks, came in and laid across the table, viewing the rocks at close range. He played appropriately with the rocks for quite some time. Then his body posture put both the educator and I on alert. It looked like he was about to throw the biggest rock of all.

My response was to ask him to help me place all the rocks into the basket and come to a short group time so I could tell them all a story about these rocks. I told the children how their teacher had played with the rocks the day before and had picked a favorite rock that she was going to keep in the room. I took that rock out and told the children how very special this rock was to their teacher. I modeled how to hold the rock oh so carefully. Then each child was invited to hold the rock, to carry it around the room, and to share it with a friend. To this day, a year or two later, the educator of this classroom remembers the impact this experience had on the children (and on her, because every time I see or speak with her she reminds me of the story). She also shared with me that the children continued to care for the rocks throughout the entire school year. An internalized lesson that speaks to a child's complex disposition can carry much positive weight in strengthening a child's spiritual development.

In observing the children's faces, body postures, and attitudes, I could honestly say that Montessori's words rang true for me. I could see that by taking care to hold the rock with utter and complete respect, the children were strengthening their inner will, control, focus, and executive functioning. While watching the children, I can better understand Montessori's claim that through such actions a radiant future might be attainable. Through such actions, beginning with the child and this new vision of early childhood education, a more peaceful world might be created (Montessori 1967).

Developing a Language for Complex Dispositions

CARING AND KINDNESS

The word *caring* means being gentle, helpful, considerate, compassionate, concerned, and loving. Caring also refers to a person's efforts to do something "correctly, safely, or without causing damage." Caring reflects a person's intent to keep oneself and others healthy and safe or to keep an object or a place in good condition.

The word *kindness* is most often defined as "the quality of being friendly, generous, and considerate."

Spiritual Development in Action

A STORY OF CARING AND KINDNESS: ZIPPING

When I was teaching pre-K and it was time to go outside, I would ask those who could zip their coats to help those who could not. This simple request accomplished multiple goals. It provided a zone of proximal development for the children who were not yet able to use a zipper because they could observe the child who was helping others and notice the steps she took to zip a coat. It set a goal for these children to learn to use a zipper themselves. It also provided positive and concrete praise to the children who had mastered using a zipper. And it demonstrated caring by offering children the opportunity to care for others by helping to zip their coats and by caring for the entire class in that we could all get outdoors more quickly. This was a classroom of four-year-olds, and by the end of the year, everyone could button and zip all by themselves.

EMPATHY AND COMPASSION

Together, caring and kindness produce empathy. Empathy is a person's ability to understand and share the feelings of another. Here is what one educator from my research study had to say:

> Children's feelings are so close to the surface—so different than adults. They tell it like it is. And they can understand on a different level. An example of that is fresh in my memory. Recently, we added a three-year-old boy, just a little bitty guy. He was adopted from a foreign country, and we think he might have some delays. He doesn't use very much language. He tries to communicate by grabbing someone or getting into somebody's space. I think one of the little girls was a little bit frightened of him. I think that's because his behavior was different than what she was used to. And she called him "that bad boy."

On another day when his mom brought him [to school], he was just crying and crying and crying. A volunteer was trying to soothe him, but it was that little girl who came over and tried to comfort him. She said to him, "I'll be your friend." It just was so sweet coming from her because I know she had some issues with this little boy. And she wasn't feeling that comfortable. And I thought, *Isn't that incredible for a child*? I think an adult might feel that they should or they might, but it wouldn't be from the heart. From this little girl, it was really from the heart. This is just such a great example of caring and empathy.

Another educator said, "You know there is research that shows that babies have sympathetic cries" and that babies will sometimes begin to cry when someone else is crying too.

Spiritual Development in Action

A STORY ABOUT CRYING

Many of my classroom observations have been in infant and toddler rooms. Sometimes I am lucky and find myself in a spiritual space where each individual is respected and truly seen. When a baby cries in such rooms, it is not uncommon to see another child move to be closer to the crying child. If you look closely at the child's face, you can see that the child is coming forward to support and encourage his friend. He may even pat his friend. These are wonderful moments of empathy.

One educator discussed the relationship between sympathy, empathy, and compassion from her point of view:

Sympathy can show understanding and kindness, but it is more pity than something that is shared. Empathy is more compassion—a deeper understanding because it is a shared experience. Sympathy—you can have compassion, but you don't necessarily share the experience. So I've seen children have a lot of contention over a toy. One child will really want a toy another child has. The child with the toy may willingly hand the toy to his peer and say, "Here, you can play with this." And the child who really wanted it shows appreciation and joy. Therefore, there was shared happiness and shared understanding between the two children. I know what it is like to want something. I know what it is like to not get it. That's the kind of empathy I'm talking about. Often people talk about empathy around some traumatic experience in one's life, but that isn't always the case. Sometimes empathy is about small matters.

REVERENCE

One other word came up when educators spoke about young children's responses to their external world. This word is *reverence*, and it was mentioned as reflecting children's ability to experience amazement and respect. One educator said, "I want every child to walk into my class knowing that I am glad they are there! Even a child having a day like *Alexander's Terrible, Horrible, No Good, Very Bad Day* should know that he or she will be respected and welcomed and hopefully helped!"

Another said, "The value system begins with the idea that every person and creation—animals, trees, and so on—has infinite value. Every time we interact and show respect for one another, help one another, it becomes an opportunity to make manifest some aspect of our own *neshama* and to relate to the *neshama* of the other. The word *neshama* means 'soul' in Hebrew and more specifically 'breath.'"

An educator from Hawaii shared that, in the schools she works in, there are three shared expectations that students and educators live by: "being kind, taking care of oneself, and taking responsibility doing your duty—doing the things you are expected to do in life."

An educator who had given a lot of thought to the concept of reverence said that she focuses on two distinct aspects of the word: reverence surrounding big questions and reverence in respect to active engagement. It is her goal to help children find balance between the two. She defined reverence as respect (meaning values and issues important for society), admiration, awe, astonishment, and amazement.

Personally, I see reverence in early childhood education as yet another means for helping children to feel transcendence similar to that which is felt when children encounter a big question that is capable of taking them beyond themselves. In relationship to reverence, the transcendence a child might feel is connected with responsibility and respect for that which is greater than himself. This type of reverence begins from a simple place—a child who picks up toys, throws away her trash, cleans up the blocks, leaves the space where she was playing clean for the next child. Children learn these acts through modeling, expectation, and loving guidance.

Too frequently, such behavior is thought to be too difficult for children or maybe not important. Sometimes it simply takes longer to invite children to help. Society's expectations of children are often so insignificant that children are given no responsibility, thus preventing adults from nurturing children's reverence and a stronger sense of self in relationship to the rest of the world. Without greater expectations, children are also receiving an indirect message that they are not capable, competent, or important enough to matter.

If you are fortunate to visit other parts of the world, you will see very young children doing amazing things. I once saw a child of three or four riding alone on the back of a camel through the hills of Jordan. I am not saying that we should all run out and have our children ride camels out in the wild; I am simply saying we should show respect to what our children are capable of doing and invite them to be part of our world—their world—rather than bystanders. When children do not learn to be responsible, life in the classroom can look and feel like chaos. So can one's home. Sometimes I visit classrooms with such chaotic environments that there is no space for spiritual moments to occur. With a sense of reverence for the classroom space and for the others in the class, a child can build strong relationships, practice mindfulness, open up to moments of wonder and joy, and also act with caring, kindness, empathy, and reverence. In such an environment, bullying cannot exist.

This type of reverence also connects the child to important cultural values. Most early childhood centers within the United States aim to support children in learning to care for themselves, for animals, and for the earth from their own personal cultural perspective. They also take steps to show great respect for each child's culture. Learning to take care of the sick is a universal value for children. This can be done by calling a classmate who has been out due to illness to see how he is feeling or maybe sending him a card. Displaying kindness, proper and decent behavior, respect for self and others, and an ability to put on a pleasant demeanor is human. This means making good choices for oneself, including choosing to be happy, not succumbing to boredom, being able to find satisfying play, making friends, and so on. Therefore, reverence can be viewed as an important bridge between a child's basic and complex dispositions.

When Spiritual Development Is Not Nurtured

During my research, I also asked educators what they thought the consequences were of *not* nurturing a young child's spiritual development. Several participants responded by saying that the child would be at risk developmentally. One educator said, "I feel that without a focus on spiritual development, a child will lose out on important psychological components in the area of social-emotional growth and certain areas in cognitive development. For example, a child might not feel secure in attachments and relationships. In cognitive development, children might lose their sense of wonder."

Another educator shared, "Children would not realize their potential or true peace and joy. [They would be] limited in their ability to experience and express empathy and compassion." These comments reflect educators' thoughts about the neglect of attachment and dispositions that occurs when a child's spiritual development is not nurtured. Other participants shared similar thoughts, as did Parker Palmer (personal communication):

> If a child's spiritual development is not addressed or nurtured, it creates a vacuum, a void, an emptiness inside that child as he or she grows older—and that emptiness may be filled by beliefs that are death-dealing rather than life-giving. There are certain questions that all human beings ask as time goes by, such as "Who am I?" "What is my purpose?" And the classic, "What is the meaning of life?" We need to understand that pathologies such as sexism, racism, xenophobia, nationalism, to say nothing of narcissism, can become "answers" to those questions if a child is not given guidance toward insights that cast light on our lives instead of leaving us in the shadows, where we are likely to do damage to others as well as to ourselves.

With words such as *sexism, racism, xenophobia, nationalism,* and *narcissism,* Parker Palmer uses a larger lens for looking at the consequences of not nurturing a child's spiritual development—a lens that affects all of society. Participants expressed a similar concern for the child's place in society.

One educator said, "Basically, I believe that if and when a child's spiritual development is not addressed or nurtured, both the child and society are shortchanged—that is, they're more likely to experience an incompleteness which may sometimes be felt as having no meaningful purpose, no zest for life, no reason to care for other living things (including people)."

Other negative consequences to society are discussed by Gamblin (2010) as paraphrased by one educator: "Research has proven that all addictions stem back to a low sense of self-worth, and the greatest protective factor against addictive and high-risk behaviors originates in the spiritual domain of infants and toddlers."

This participant looked at self-esteem and self-worth through the lens of a specific ideology:

> We read books written by an author who lived a hundred years ago. She differentiated between self-esteem and self-worth. Now when you go to the research, the research today is showing that self-esteem can have very detrimental impact on the individual character development, because self-esteem tends to elevate yourself above others and is tied to pride and selfishness. The psychological research that has come out within the last fifteen to twenty years is saying the same thing, whereas self-worth is valuing others as you value yourself.

Another participant said, "I think there are consequences for society, as well. The spiritual child—or the child whose spiritual development has been nurtured—is more likely to contribute to the establishment of a more spiritual society, a society where empathy, caring, compassion, and peace are valued." Another participant added, "Children whose moral and spiritual developments are not nurtured are at risk of not recognizing the role they play in creating a world that is just and beautiful for all. That lack of awareness strikes me as a very lonely and isolating condition."

Once again, a participant ends the conversation with a sense of hope. She said, "Every child is worth all the love we can bestow on them. If even the angriest child is treated with love and kindness, that child is given an opportunity for spiritual experiences; I have to feel that it must help. I think that is the hope that needs to be in every teacher—the courage to always persist."

If we do not persist and children are not given opportunities for spiritual experiences, we are left with this:

Participants' views about the consequences of failure to nurture spiritual development

It can shortchange both the child and society.

It can create feelings of anger that results in addiction.

It can leave a child with a low sense of self-worth.

It can lead to nationalistic chauvinism and religious extremism.

It can create in children and society a vacuum, a void, and an emptiness inside.

It can lead to narcissism.

It can weaken a child's moral development.

It can place a child at risk of not realizing his or her own potential, thus living a life that is not complete.

It can cause a child to feel lonely and isolated.

It can prevent a child from knowing true peace and joy.

It can limit a child's ability to experience and express empathy and compassion.

It can lead to gangs and bullying.

Conclusion: Raising Kind Children Who Don't Bully

Educators, parents, caregivers, politicians, and lawmakers all have a choice, and so do children. We can all work on strengthening our own spiritual development, nurturing the spiritual development of others, and taking time to act with care, kindness, empathy, and reverence toward others. Having a new, usable definition of *spiritual development* will help to create a stronger beginning for all children, one in which caring, kindness, empathy, and reverence overpower narcissism, hatred, and cruelty. In such an environment, bullying simply will not and cannot exist.

THINGS TO DO TO ENCOURAGE KINDNESS
INSTEAD OF BULLYING IN THE CLASSROOM

☼ We must do all we can to support the emergence of complex dispositions.

— Look for children as they act with kindness, empathy, and reverence.

— Give these complex dispositions names so that children can both recognize and discuss them with others.

— "It was so kind of you to help zip your friend's coat."

— "When you hugged your crying friend, you showed empathy."

☼ Expect children to grow in their ability to will themselves to do what is right and good. If we do not expect this of children, it may never happen.

☼ Expect children to ask big questions that you will not answer but will explore together.

☼ Remember to encourage awareness of and appreciation for the uniqueness that exists between people and throughout the world.

☼ Create a shared sense of reverence . . .

— so that children can build strong relationships and practice mindfulness;

— so that children can open up to moments of wonder and joy; and

— so that children can act with caring, kindness, empathy, and reverence.

☼ See children as authentically competent and capable, and because of this, have expectations and responsibilities for them. Give them important jobs to do around the classroom:

— Keep books neat.

— Return blocks to the shelves in an orderly fashion.

— Be responsible for plants, cleanup, pets, and so on.

— Take good care of crayons, paint, and paper.

☼ Have high but reachable expectations for children's behavior.

— Create classroom expectations together with the children that state what they *should* be doing, not what they can't do.

— Kindness should be an expectation.

— If children misbehave, find ways to help them get back on track.

— Find ways to help children learn how to self-regulate their own behavior.

— With infants, this self-regulation begins with modeling.

— With toddlers, self-regulation is modeled through both actions and words directed at the children involved. You might take a child's hand and show her how to politely say, "I would like that toy when you are done."

— Beyond these ages, children should be expected to grow in their ability to follow the norms of a classroom.

A Stronger Beginning Begins Now

REGAINING A LANGUAGE of spiritual development that begins with infants and young children and those who care for them can help move the United States closer to the "good society" Howard Gardner, Amitai Etzioni, and Maria Montessori mentioned. Such a society is difficult to build without starting at the beginning. This book ends with hope for the future: that early childhood educators can provide a stronger beginning for young children by honoring their spiritual development.

A Working Definition of Spiritual Development

All the pieces are now in place to put forth a working definition of spiritual development. It is a definition that is intended to be comfortable and supportive for all people, especially very young children attending public early childhood programs.

The concept of spiritual development has always been around, but it has not always been visible or distinct enough for educators and parents to use with their children. Often, the term has referred to God and religion. Now it is time for us to acknowledge the presence of spiritual development from a different perspective—to recognize its potential in helping all children grow and develop into well-functioning and compassionate human beings.

Phase 1: The First Stages

LOVE, CONNECTION, AND A POSITIVE SENSE OF SELF

This definition of spiritual development begins as most developmental theories do: as stage development or stage theory. This means that steps are required to move forward, with one step building upon another. The first stage begins with love. Almost all early childhood educators today understand the concepts of love and attachment as they relate to young children. What is new in this discussion is that this love ignites the spiritual embryo and awakens the child's absorbent mind. Each child's spiritual embryo works as a force to propel the child forward, allowing him to feel love, make connections, and develop a sense of self. If the child's first encounter is with someone who sees the child with loving eyes, then this child's spirit will continue to flourish. If not, the child's spiritual development will be compromised. It is through acts of love that a child begins to develop his initial sense of self. The child will achieve a positive inner recognition of himself.

SPIRITUAL EMBRYO

Once a child begins the realization of self, still most likely in an unconscious state, the child will continue on a lifelong journey in relationship building. Strong and loving relationships are built when a child's spiritual development is nurtured. The child's spiritual development is continuously strengthened via strong and loving relationships and deep connections.

This is the stage in which Martin Buber's concept of I-Thou is helpful in describing the power of relationships, whether the child's relationship is with another living creature or a nonliving thing. Without this foundation of deep relationships, the child's spiritual development is further compromised.

Love, Connections, and
Relationships Lead to a
Positive Sense of Self

BASIC DISPOSITIONS, SPIRITUAL MOMENTS, AND FEELINGS OF WONDER, AWE, JOY, AND INNER PEACE

The next stage in the definition looks at a child's disposition. At first I saw these dispositions as similar to those defined by Lilian Katz and Stephen Katz (2009) as a child's nature, character, and temperament. But as I read and reread the data, I realized that there is a depth to young children's dispositions, indicating that these dispositions are internal, deeply connected to each individual child, and possibly present at birth. I labeled these *basic dispositions*. They parallel what some might call one's *personal essence* or *born personality*, which differs from character in that character can and should be guided and changed. Each child has a unique set of dispositions that needs to be seen, acknowledged, and appreciated by a close and loving adult. This gives the adult the knowledge and insight she needs to purposely provide an environment filled with spiritual moments that match the child's dispositions. These steps help to guarantee that the child will experience moments of wonder, joy, awe, and peace at least a portion of each day. It is during such moments that a child's spiritual development is being nurtured. Spiritual moments also provide time for young children to engage in quality experiences with others, with themselves, in and with nature, in complex relationships, and with big questions. This is where children have great opportunities to continuously learn about themselves and the world through all their senses and through their entire beings.

STAGE 2

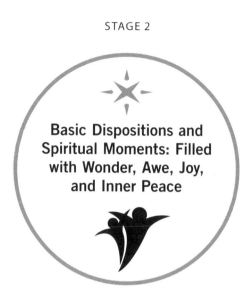

Basic Dispositions and Spiritual Moments: Filled with Wonder, Awe, Joy, and Inner Peace

COMPLEX DISPOSITIONS AND ACTS OF CARING, KINDNESS, EMPATHY, AND REVERENCE

The final stage in nurturing spiritual development has to do with developing a child's "complex dispositions." Complex dispositions become evident when children have the power, reasoning, or simply the reflexes to act with care, kindness, empathy, and reverence toward others, themselves, and the world around them. In other words, complex dispositions are positive external responses that emerge after a child has experienced feelings that have strengthened their basic dispositions. Here is an example of how this works. A young child experiences joy. This nurtures the child's basic disposition and leads to personal feelings that "I am good, worthy, competent, and capable." These feelings, in turn, lead the child to react or respond in positive ways to external stimuli or situations that might occur. As the child grows older, values, morals, and a sense of duty and responsibility toward others eventually emerge from the child's complex dispositions. Complex dispositions are all about children finding their place and their role in the world and growing in their ability to make good choices. A child developing complex dispositions will learn and internalize ideas such as cause and effect, consequences, and the importance of being responsible, as well as the role these play in helping her to make decisions, make and keep connections, and manage her own behavior.

STAGE 3

Complex Dispositions:
Acts of Caring, Kindness,
Empathy, and Reverence

The System of Spiritual Development

Spiritual development becomes a system once all three stages are in place. A system is defined as "parts or subsystems collected and used for a common goal." Systems are also self-sustaining. The system of spiritual development is composed of subsystems that consist of stage 1: Love, Connection, and a Positive Sense of Self; stage 2: Basic Dispositions, Spiritual Moments, and Feelings of Wonder, Awe, Joy, and Inner Peace; and stage 3: Complex Dispositions and Acts of Caring, Kindness, Empathy, and Reverence. When

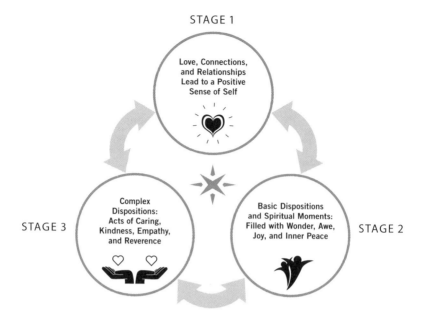

Love, Connections, and Relationships Lead to a Positive Sense of Self

Complex Dispositions: Acts of Caring, Kindness, Empathy, and Reverence

STAGE 3

Basic Dispositions and Spiritual Moments: Filled with Wonder, Awe, Joy, and Inner Peace

STAGE 2

In this system, the arrows go in all directions, indicating that spiritual development can be nurtured in many ways throughout one's lifetime.

these stages work together, the system of spiritual development becomes self-sustaining. I believe that this shift from stage development to system development can take place at a very young age if a child's spirituality is nurtured beginning at birth. Although more research is required in order to make this a definitive statement, I hypothesize that a system of spiritual development might exist before a child reaches six months old and definitely before one year old.

Here are a few examples of how the system of spiritual development sustains itself:

SCENARIO 1

A child makes a new friend. In other words, a new connection is made (stage 1). This creates an opening for the child to feel moments of joy and happiness (stage 2), which then helps the child to act kindly (stage 3), such as saying hello to someone who looks lonely. This might even lead to making another new friend (stage 1).

SCENARIO 2

A little girl went for a walk with her grandmother. The grandmother knew that this child loves colors and flowers, so they walked to a rose garden. The little girl was filled with wonder and awe at seeing such beautiful and colorful flowers (stage 2). The grandmother and granddaughter had a great time together (stage 1). Later that day, the little girl offered to help her mother get dinner ready (stage 3).

SCENARIO 3

A child saw that a friend was sad and sat down to be with her, thus demonstrating empathy (stage 3). Throughout the rest of the day, the child who had displayed empathy felt good inside; a sliver of joy stayed with her (stage 2). Because of this, she was less timid and tried working with clay for the first time (stage 1).

Where is spiritual development within these examples? Spiritual development is being nurtured during these moments. It is occurring inside the children. It is reflected in the children's social, emotional, cognitive, and physical responses to life itself. Spiritual development affects the entire child, not just the parts but the whole, and in so doing helps to sustain a more integrated human being.

The Ultimate Outcome of Spiritual Nurturing: Creating a Better World

The initial goal for defining spiritual development of young children was to revisit and renew a language for early childhood educators, parents, and caregivers to use so that spiritual development could once again become an acknowledged and respected part of human development. Second, having a working definition of spiritual development as a system offers educators, parents, and caregivers the opportunity to practice nurturing a child's spiritual development within a public setting. The most important reason for inviting spiritual development back into the culture of the United States is the potential to nurture children who will know, understand, and appreciate

how to become good citizens; people who seek relationships, appreciate wonder, and act with kindness; and people who will grow in their abilities to make ethical and moral decisions.

Next Steps: Ideas to Help Parents and Educators Nurture Children's Spiritual Development

1 Ignite children's spiritual embryos by offering unconditional and authentic love, appreciation, and respect to every single child.

2 Truly see the child, really know the child, and honestly support the child in knowing herself.

3 Begin to use the language of spiritual development:

☼ *self-awareness* instead of *self-esteem*

☼ basic dispositions fed by spiritual moments in which a child is filled with wonder, awe, joy, and inner peace

☼ complex dispositions: a child's inner dispositions made visible to the outside world through moments of caring, kindness, empathy, and reverence

4   Provide beautiful spaces so that spiritual moments are plentiful.

5   Expect every child to be respectful and responsible to those around her, which includes self, other people, the earth, the classroom environment, a child's bedroom, and the streets and neighborhoods in which the child lives.

6   Learn more about spiritual development and its relationship to all developmental domains. If spiritual development is the foundation for all learning, investing time to know more about it for yourself and your children/students is important.

7   Find ways to nurture your own spiritual development.

Additional Questions to Ponder and Research

1   What is the connection between spiritual development and the other domains of development, such as cognitive, social, emotional, and physical development? The belief of the participants of this study is that spiritual development guides all other areas of development, but replication and further analysis would be beneficial.

2   How might early childhood practices look if the definition of spiritual development as established in this study were applied to early childhood education programs? How would deep connections and spiritual moments occur within the development of each existing developmental domain? What would be the long-term implications of applying this theoretical framework to practice and research in early childhood?

3   What is the relationship between spiritual development, moral development, character building, faith development, and the cultivation of values? The findings suggest that there are additional complex dispositions to be developed. When and how do these additional complex dispositions come into existence?

4   How does spiritual development manifest itself in a variety of cultural contexts and religious groups? Such studies have the potential to provide additional information on spiritual development.

Today, in a world filled with rapid changes and uncertainty, thinking about what we truly want for our children is vital. I know I am not alone when I dream of supporting the development of the whole child, meaning children who are intellectually strong, socially and emotionally stable, physically fit, and spiritually sound. My hope is that this book will help to place the concept of spiritual development back into educational philosophy, as it has proven to be an important ingredient for raising whole children and for helping make the world a good place, a better place, for us all to live.

References

Änggård, Eva. 2010. "Making Use of 'Nature' in an Outdoor Preschool: Classroom, Home and Fairyland." *Children, Youth and Environments* 20 (1): 4–25.

Armitage, Kevin C. 2009. *The Nature Study Movement: The Forgotten Popularizer of America's Conservation Ethic*. Lawrence: University of Kansas Press.

Bailie, Patti Ensel. 2012. "Connecting Children to Nature: A Multiple Case Study of Nature Center Preschools." PhD diss., University of Nebraska–Lincoln. http://digitalcommons.unl.edu/cgi/viewcontent.cgi?article=1028&context=teachlearnstudent.

Bazelon, Emily. 2013. *Sticks and Stones: Defeating the Culture of Bullying and Rediscovering the Power of Character and Empathy*. New York: Random House.

Bowlby, John. 1951. *Maternal Care and Mental Health*. Geneva: World Health Organization.

Bretherton, Inge. 1992. "The Origins of Attachment Theory: John Bowlby and Mary Ainsworth." *Developmental Psychology* 28 (5): 759–75.

Bronfenbrenner, Urie. 1971. *Report to the President: White House Conference on Children*. Washington, DC: US Government Printing Office.

———. 1973. *Two Worlds of Childhood: U.S. and U.S.S.R.* New York: Pocket Books.

Buber, Martin. (1923) 1996. *I and Thou*. Translated by Walter Kaufmann. New York: Touchstone.

Carson, Rachel. 1962. *Silent Spring*. Boston: Houghton Mifflin.

Center on the Developing Child. 2017. "Toxic Stress." Harvard University. Accessed March 17. http://developingchild.harvard.edu/science/key-concepts/toxic-stress.

Chawla, Louise. 2012. "The Importance of Access to Nature for Young Children." *Early Childhood Matters* 118 (June): 48–51. https://bernardvanleer.org/app/uploads/2015/12/ECM118_Living-conditions-The-influence-on-young-childrens-health.pdf.

Chein, Rochel. 2016. "Which Blessing Is Said upon Seeing a Rainbow?" Accessed December 31. www.chabad.org/parshah/article_cdo/aid/931633/jewish/Which-blessing-is-said-upon-seeing-a-rainbow.htm.

Coles, Robert. 1990. *The Spiritual Life of Children*. Boston: Houghton Mifflin.

Cooper, Bridget, and Paul Brna. 2002. "Supporting High Quality Interaction and Motivation in the Classroom Using ICT: The Social and Emotional Learning and Engagement in the NIMIS Project." *Education, Communication & Information* 2 (2–3): 113–38.

Copple, Carol, and Sue Bredekamp, eds. 2009. *Developmentally Appropriate Practice in Early Childhood Programs*. Washington, DC: NAEYC.

Cowan, Megan. 2010. "Tips for Teaching Mindfulness to Kids." Greater Good Science Center, University of California–Berkley. http://greatergood.berkeley.edu/article /item/tips_for_teaching_mindfulness_to_kids.

Curtis, Deb, and Margie Carter. 2015. *Designs for Living and Learning: Transforming Early Childhood Environments*. Rev. ed. St. Paul, MN: Redleaf Press.

Dewey, John. (1916) 2005. *Democracy and Education: An Introduction to the Philosophy of Education*. New York: Barnes & Noble.

Donaldson, Julia. 1999. *The Gruffalo*. New York: Dial Books for Young Readers.

Earth Charter Initiative. 2017. "Earth Charter." Accessed March 17. http://earthcharter .org/discover/the-earth-charter.

Erickson, Deanna M., and Julie A. Ernst. 2011. "The Real Benefits of Nature Play Every Day." *Exchange* 33 (4): 97–99.

Etzioni, Amitai. 2001. *Next: The Road to the Good Society*. New York: Basic Books.

Fowler, James W. 1995. *Stages of Faith: The Psychology of Human Development and the Quest for Meaning*. New York: HarperCollins.

Gamblin, Rose Tooley. 2010. *Like a Little Child: The Spiritual Journey of Infants and Toddlers*. Smithsburg, MD: MRG Media.

Gandini, Lella. 2013. Foreword to *Nature Education with Young Children: Integrating Inquiry and Practice*, edited by Daniel R. Meier and Stephanie Sisk-Hilton. New York: Routledge.

Gandini, Lella, Lynn Hill, Louise Cadwell, and Charles Schwall, eds. 2005. *In the Spirit of the Studio: Learning from the Atelier of Reggio Emilia*. New York: Teachers College Press.

Gardner, Howard. 1993. *Multiple Intelligences: The Theory in Practice*. New York: Basic Books.

———. 1999. *Intelligence Reframed: Multiple Intelligences for the 21st Century*. New York: Basic Books.

———. 2006. *Multiple Intelligences: New Horizons*. Rev. ed. New York: Basic Books.

Gardner, Howard, Mihaly Csikszentmihalyi, and William Damon. 2001. *Good Work: When Excellence and Ethics Meet*. New York: Basic Books.

Green, Arthur. 2001. "Neshamah." In *The Jewish Lights Spirituality Handbook: A Guide to Understanding, Exploring & Living a Spiritual Life*, edited by Stuart M. Matlins. Woodstock, VT: Jewish Lights.

Greenland, Susan Kaiser. 2010. *The Mindful Child: How to Help Your Kid Manage Stress and Become Happier, Kinder, and More Compassionate*. New York: Free Press.

Handelman, Maxine Segal, and Deborah L. Schein. 2004. *What's Jewish about Butterflies? 36 Dynamic, Engaging Lessons for the Early Childhood Classroom*. Denver: A.R.E. Publishing.

Harris, Kathleen I. 2007. "Re-conceptualizing Spirituality in the Light of Educating Young Children." *International Journal of Children's Spirituality* 12 (3): 263–75.

Hart, Tobin. 2006. "Spiritual Experiences and Capacities of Children and Youth." In *The Handbook of Spiritual Development in Childhood and Adolescence*, edited by Eugene C. Roehlkepartain, Pamela Ebstyne King, Linda Wagener, and Peter L. Benson, 163–78. Thousand Oaks, CA: Sage Publications.

Heschel, Abraham Joshua. 1955. *God in Search of Man: A Philosophy of Judaism*. New York: Farrar, Straus & Cudahy.

Honig, Alice S. 2002. *Secure Relationships: Nurturing Infant/Toddler Attachment in Early Care Settings*. Washington, DC: NAEYC.

Jensen, Eric. 2008. *Brain-Based Learning: The New Paradigm of Teaching*. 2nd ed. Thousand Oaks, CA: Corwin Press.

Kagan, Jerome. 2004. "The Uniquely Human in Human Nature." *Daedalus* 133 (4): 77–88.

Katz, Lilian G., and Stephen J. Katz. 2009. *Intellectual Emergencies: Some Reflections on Mothering and Teaching*. Louisville, NC: K Press.

Kellert, Stephen R. 2005. *Building for Life: Designing and Understanding the Human–Nature Connection*. Washington, DC: Island Press.

Kirmani, Mubina Hassanali, and Sanaullah Kirmani. 2009. "Recognition of Seven Spiritual Identities and Its Implications on Children." *Journal of Children's Spirituality* 14 (4): 369–83.

Lally, J. Ronald, Peter Mangione, and Deborah Greenwald, eds. 2006. *Concepts for Care: 20 Essays on Infant/Toddler Development and Learning*. San Francisco: WestEd.

Langer, Ellen J. 2014. *Mindfulness*. Boston: Da Capo Press.

Leutenberg, Ester R.A., and Deborah L. Schein. 2017. *Nurturing Spiritual Development in Children by Understanding Our Own Spirituality*. Duluth, MN: Whole Person.

Louv, Richard. 2005. *Last Child in the Woods*. Chapel Hill, NC: Algonquin Books.

———. 2011. *The Nature Principle: Human Restoration and the End of Nature-Deficit Disorder*. Chapel Hill, NC: Algonquin Books.

Mata, Jennifer. 2010. "Children's Spirituality as Experienced and Expressed in a Kindergarten Classroom." PhD diss., Teachers College, Columbia University, NY. https://eric.ed.gov/?id=ED518920.

Meier, Daniel R., and Stephanie Sisk-Hilton, eds. 2013. *Nature Education with Young Children: Integrating Inquiry and Practice*. New York: Routledge.

Montessori, Maria. 1963. *The Secret of Childhood*. Translated by Barbara Barclay Carter. Bombay, India: Orient Longmans.

———. 1967. *The Absorbent Mind*. Translated by Claude A. Claremont. New York: Holt, Rinehart and Winston.

Moore, Robin, and Clare Cooper Marcus. 2008. "Healthy Planet, Healthy Children: Designing Nature into the Daily Spaces of Childhood." In *Biophilic Design: The Theory, Science, and Practice of Bringing Buildings to Life*, edited by Stephen R. Kellert, Judith H. Heerwagen, and Martin L. Mador, 153–203. Hoboken, NJ: Wiley.

Nell, Marcia L., Walter F. Drew, and Deborah E. Bush. 2013. *From Play to Practice: Connecting Teachers' Play to Children's Learning*. Washington, DC: NAEYC.

Newberg, Andrew B., and Stephanie K. Newberg. 2006. "A Neuropsychological Perspective on Spiritual Development." In *The Handbook of Spiritual Development in Childhood and Adolescence*, edited by Eugene C. Roehlkepartain, Pamela Ebstyne King, Linda Wagener, and Peter L. Benson, 183–96. Thousand Oaks, CA: Sage Publications.

Noddings, Nel. 2007. *Happiness and Education*. New York: Cambridge University.

Pestalozzi, Johann Heinrich. 1898. *Letters on Early Education*. Syracuse, NY: C. W. Bardeen.

Phenice, Lillian A., and Robert J. Griffore. 2003. "Young Children and the Natural World." *Contemporary Issues in Early Childhood* 4 (2): 167–71.

Raikes, Helen H., and Carolyn Pope Edwards. 2009. *Extending the Dance in Infant and Toddler Caregiving: Enhancing Attachment and Relationships*. Baltimore: Paul H. Brookes.

Rimm, Sylvia B. 2008. *How to Parent So Children Will Learn: Strategies for Raising Happy, Achieving Children*. Scottsdale, AZ: Great Potential Press.

Rinaldi, Carlina. 2006. *In Dialogue with Reggio Emilia: Listening, Researching and Learning*. New York: Routledge.

Rivkin, Mary S. 2013. *The Great Outdoors: Advocating for Natural Spaces for Young Children*. Rev. ed. With Deborah L. Schein. Washington, DC: NAEYC.

Schein, Deborah L. 2012. "Early Childhood Educators' Perceptions of Spiritual Development in Young Children: A Social Constructivist Grounded Theory Study." PhD diss., Walden University. ProQuest (3547107).

———. 2014. "Nature's Role in Children's Spiritual Development." *Children, Youth and Environments* 24 (2): 78–101.

Schein, Jeffrey. 2009. "Towards Thick Description of Teaching and Learning Jewish Texts: A Schwabian Perspective." Unpublished paper, Siegal College, Cleveland, OH.

Schwab, Joseph J. 1969. "The Practical: A Language for Curriculum." *School Review* 78 (1): 1–23.

Semrud-Clikeman, Margaret. 2017. "Research in Brain Function and Learning: The Importance of Matching Instruction to a Child's Maturity Level." American Psychological Association. Accessed May 1. http://www.apa.org/education/k12/brain-function.aspx.

Senge, Peter M. 1990. *The Fifth Discipline: The Art and Practice of the Learning Organization*. New York: Doubleday/Currency.

Shafer, William M. 2004. "The Infant as Reflection of Soul: The Time before There Was a Self." *Zero to Three* 24 (3): 4–8.

Shonkoff, Jack P., and Deborah A. Phillips, eds. 2000. *From Neurons to Neighborhoods: The Science of Early Child Development*. Washington, DC: National Academy Press.

Siegel, Daniel J. 2010. *Mindsight: The New Science of Personal Transformation*. New York: Bantam Books.

Snow, Kyle. 2016. "Research News You Can Use: Debunking the Play vs. Learning Dichotomy." Accessed October 20. www.naeyc.org/content/research-news-you-can-use-play-vs-learning.

Sobel, David, ed. 2016. *Nature Preschools and Forest Kindergartens: The Handbook for Outdoor Learning*. St. Paul, MN: Redleaf Press.

Surr, John. 2011. "Links between Early Attachment Experiences and Manifestations of Spirituality." *International Journal of Children's Spirituality* 16 (2): 129–41.

Taylor, Andrea Faber, Frances E. Kuo, and William C. Sullivan. 2002. "Views of Nature and Self-Discipline: Evidence from Inner City Children." *Journal of Environmental Psychology* 22 (1–2): 49–63.

Vygotsky, Lev S. 1962. *Thought and Language*. Translated by Eugenia Hanfmann and Gertrude Vakar. Cambridge, MA: MIT Press.

———. 1978. *Mind in Society: The Development of Higher Psychological Processes*. Cambridge, MA: Harvard University Press.

Wilson, Edward O. 1984. *Biophilia*. Cambridge, MA: Harvard University Press.

Wilson, Ruth A. 2014. *Nature and Young Children: Encouraging Creative Play and Learning in Natural Environments*. 2nd ed. New York: Routledge.

Wilson, Ruth A., and Deborah L. Schein. 2017. "Supporting the Spiritual Development of Young Children." *Child Care Exchange* 39 (2): 26–32.

Wittmer, Donna Sasse, and Sandra H. Petersen. 2014. *Infant and Toddler Development and Responsive Program Planning: A Relationship-Based Approach*. 3rd ed. Boston: Pearson.

Index

child's basic disposition and
    baking cookies example, 64–65
    blocks example, 63
    fairy tea party example, 64
    travel example, 66
as essential part of milieu, 69
imagination in
    as essential part of milieu, 69
    spiritual development and, 68, 70
importance of child's choice of, 65, 66
learning and, 45, 52, 66, 97
Ploof, Robin, 51–52
pluralism in teaching, 115
The Practical (Schwab), 55–56
praise
    dangers of inappropriate/excessive, 28,
        29–31
    importance of authentic and appropriate, 31
    offering honest, 32
provocation, 21

Reggio Emilia philosophy
    construction of knowledge by children,
        86–87
    Hundred Languages of Children, 44
    milieu as educator, 96
    provocation, 21
    teacher researchers, 46
relationships
    balance between self and others in, 29, 30
    developing loving, 20
    disposition and, 61
    elements of positive, 56
        respect, 30, 35
        trust, 11–12
    getting to know child's disposition and,
        57–58
    importance of sharing experiences, 88
    infant's need to establish, 24–25, 27–28
    modeling done in, 22
    with nature, 74
        actions to nurture, 89–90
        with others and, 106
    as necessary to learning experience, 40, 56

peace and, 88–89
Pestalozzi's four spheres, 13–14
sense of self and, 106
spiritual moments in, 106–109
strengthened by spiritual development,
    134
See also I-Thou relationships
resilience, examples of, 17
respect
    as basis of love and attachment, 16
    for child's disposition, 32
    as element of positive relationships, 30, 35
    reverence and, 96, 125
    in STREAMS, 48, 52
    trust and, 12
responsibility
    actions to encourage, 131
    nature and, 85
    reverence and, 125–126
    sense of self and, 13–14, 88
    in STREAMS, 48, 52
    trust and, 12
reverence, 96, 123–126, 131
Rimm, Sylvia, 31
routine, importance of, 97
ruach (spirit), uniqueness of individual's, 18
Rubel, Nance, 77

safety and security, importance of, 16
Scheffler, Axel, 84
Schein, Deborah L., 5, 21
Schwab, Joseph, 55–56
self-awareness
    awareness-sensing and, 82–83
    versus self-esteem, 28, 29–30
self-esteem
    effect of excessive praise, 30–31
    versus self-awareness, 28, 29–30
    self-worth versus, 128
Selly, Patty Born, 51–52
Senge, Peter, 114
sense of order
    creation of spiritual moments and, 111
    space and, 95, 96